Love UX design ! 2/11/15

Praise for *Lean UX*

"Customer Development and Lean Startup changed the way businesses are built, because even the smartest teams can't predict market and user behavior. This book brings both methodologies to UX so you can build cheaper, faster, and—most importantly—better experiences."

Alex Osterwalder—Author and Entrepreneur;
Cofounder, Business Model Foundry GmbH

"Many UX designers I know fear the words 'Agile' or 'Lean' out of fear that they threaten their creative process and lower the quality standards of their work. But with more and more software development teams adopting these methodologies, it's important that the UX team embrace this change and find ways to use the system to its advantage. In this book, Jeff Gothelf and Josh Seiden explain what Lean UX is, why you should practice it, and how it can help you and your team build better products (which is what it's all about, right?). Using these principles, the RunKeeper team has broken down the traditional barriers between engineering and UX and has made everyone responsible for creating an incredible user experience."

Tom Boates—VP, User Experience, RunKeeper

"There is a revolution afoot. It is the move away from big design up front and isolated, specialized teams throwing documents over the wall to each other. Applying the principles of Lean startups, Jeff and Josh lay out the principles of Lean UX, which can literally transform the way you bring experiences to life. I have firsthand experience applying their wisdom and am excited about taking Agile to the next level. Get this book. But most importantly, put this book into practice."

Bill Scott—Sr. Director, User Interface Engineering, PayPal, Inc.

Lean UX

Applying Lean Principles to Improve User Experience

Jeff Gothelf

Josh Seiden, editor

O'REILLY®

Beijing · Cambridge · Farnham · Köln · Sebastopol · Tokyo

Lean UX
by Jeff Gothelf

Published by O'Reilly Media, Inc., 1005 Gravenstein Highway North, Sebastopol, CA 95472.

O'Reilly books may be purchased for educational, business, or sales promotional use. Online editions are also available for most titles (*http://my.safaribooksonline.com*). For more information, contact our corporate/institutional sales department: (800) 998-9938 or *corporate@oreilly.com*.

Acquisitions Editor: Mary Treseler	**Indexer:** Lucie Haskins
Developmental Editor: Josh Seiden	**Compositor:** Holly Bauer
Production Editor: Holly Bauer	**Cover Designer:** Mark Paglietti
Copyeditor: Nancy Kotary	**Interior Designer:** Ron Bilodeau
Proofreader: Jilly Gagnon	**Illustrator:** Kara Ebrahim

March 2013: First Edition.

Revision History for the First Edition:

2013-02-08	First release
2013-03-08	Second release

See *http://oreilly.com/catalog/errata.csp?isbn=0636920021827* for release details.

ISBN: 978-1-449-31165-0
[CW]

For Carrie, Grace, and Sophie

Contents

SECTION I: INTRODUCTION AND PRINCIPLES

SECTION II: PROCESS

SECTION III: MAKING IT WORK

Foreword

In reading *Lean UX*, you're about to embark on a tour of a new way of working. For those of us steeped in traditional management techniques, it may seem a little disorienting. I sometimes like to imagine what it would be like to have a birds-eye view of the typical modern corporation. From on high, you could examine each silo of functional excellence one at a time. See them in your mind's eye: Marketing, Operations, Manufacturing, IT, Engineering, Design, and on and on in a tidy row of crisp, well-run silos.

Let's imagine you reached down to grab one of these silos and popped its top off to see inside. What would you see? This being a modern company, you'd see each silo designed for maximum efficiency. To achieve this efficiency, you'd likely find a highly iterative, customer-centric approach to problem solving. In Manufacturing, you'd encounter traditional lean thinking. In Engineering or IT, perhaps some variation on agile development. In Marketing, customer development. In Operations, DevOps. And of course in Design, the latest in design thinking, interaction design, and user research techniques.

Zooming back out to our high perch, we might be forgiven for thinking "This company uses a variety of rigorous, hypothesis-driven, customer-centric, and iterative methodologies. Surely, it must be an extremely agile company, capable of reacting quickly to changes in market conditions and continuously innovating!" But those of us who work in modern companies know how far this is from the truth.

How is it possible that our departmental silos are operating with agility, but our companies are hopelessly rigid and slow? From our far-off vantage point, we have missed something essential. Although our departments may value agility, the *interconnections* between them are still mired in an antiquated industrial past.

Consider just one example, which I hope will sound familiar. A company decides it must innovate to survive. It commissions a design team (either in-house or external) to investigate the future of its industry and recommend innovative new products that could secure its future. A period of great excitement commences. Customers are interviewed, observed, analyzed. Experiments, surveys, focus groups, prototypes and smoke tests follow one after the other. Concepts are rapidly conceived, tested, rejected, and refined.

And what happens at the end of this process? The designers proudly present—and the businesses enthusiastically celebrates—a massive specification document with their findings and recommendations. The iteration, experimentation, and discovery ceases. Now engineering is called upon to execute this plan. And although the engineering process may be agile, the specification document is rigidly fixed. What happens if the engineers discover that the specification was unworkable or even slightly flawed? What if the concepts worked great in the lab but have no commercial appeal? What if market conditions have changed since the original "learning" took place?

I once spoke to a company who had commissioned—at terrible expense—a multi-year study of their industry. The result was an impressive "view of the future" display custom-built into their corporate headquarters. Inside this room, you could see an extrapolation of what the next 10 years would look like in their industry, complete with working demos of futuristic product concepts. You can guess what happened over the succeeding 10 years: absolutely nothing. The company rotated hundreds or thousands of executives, managers, and workers through this glimpse of the future. And in fact, 10 years later, the room no longer looks futuristic. Against all odds, its forecasts turned out to be largely accurate. And yet, the company had failed to commercialize even one of the recommendations in the attendant specification document. So I asked the company what they planned to do next; they told me they were going back to the original designers and asking them to forecast the next 10 years! The company blamed their engineers and managers for their failure to commercialize, not the designers.

When I tell this story to nondesigners, they are horrified and want to convince me that it is the fancy design firm who is to blame. When I tell it to senior executives—in both large companies and startups alike—they cringe. They are constantly deluged with complaints from every single function that they are fast and cutting edge but it is the other departments that slow the company down. When the whole company fails to find new sources of growth, there is plenty of blame to go around.

But the fault is not with the designers, or the engineers, or even the executives. The problem is the systems we use to build companies. We are still building linear organizations in a world that demands constant change. We are still building silos in a world that demands thorough collaboration. And we are still investing in analysis, arguing over specifications, and efficiently producing deliverables in a world that demands continuous experimentation in order to achieve continuous innovation.

It has been just about four years since I first began writing and speaking about a new concept called Lean Startup, and barely a year since I published *The Lean Startup: How Today's Entrepreneurs Use Continuous Innovation to Achieve Radically Successful Businesses* (Crown Business). In that time, I have seen the ideas grow and spread—from industry to industry, sector to sector, and function to function. Every time we have encountered new terrain, we have relied on farsighted leaders to help translate the core principles and develop new processes to implement them.

Lean UX is an important step in that evolution. For the first time, we have a comprehensive look at how Lean Startup principles apply in a design context. Along the way, it introduces important new tools and techniques to achieve superior collaboration, faster delivery, and—most importantly— dramatically better products.

Lean Startup is a big tent. It builds on established ideas from many disciplines, from lean manufacturing to design thinking. It gives us a common vocabulary and set of concepts that can be used to accelerate results across the whole company. We can stop wasting time arguing about who is to blame and which department should rule the day.

It is my hope that all of us will remember to heed Jeff Gothelf's call to "get out of the deliverables business" and return our focus where it belongs, enlisting the whole corporation in its most urgent task: delighting customers.

It is time to break down the silos, unite the clans, and get to work.

Eric Ries
January 30, 2013
San Francisco, CA

Preface

The biggest lie in software is Phase II.

If you've spent any time building digital products in the last 20 years—regardless of your role—you've felt the sting of this lie. You set aside features and ideas for the next phase of work and then they are gone, never to be heard from again. As a designer, I've had hundreds, if not thousands, of wireframes and workflows end up in this same bucket.

But did these ideas disappear because they were flawed? Did the features that shipped actually meet customer and business goals, so Phase II ideas were never needed? Or did the team simply run out of time? The team never got to Phase II.

In *The Lean Startup*, Eric Ries lays out his vision for how to ensure that the ideas that have the most value get the most resources. The method Ries promotes relies on experimentation, rapid iteration of ideas, and evolutionary processes. For Ries, the entire concept of Phase II becomes moot.

The junction of Lean Startup and User Experience-based (UX) design—and their symbiotically coexistence—is *Lean UX*.

What Is Lean UX and How Is It Different?

The Lean principles underlying Lean Startup apply to Lean UX in three ways. First, they help us remove waste from our UX design process. We move away from heavily documented handoffs to a process that creates only the design artifacts we need to move the team's learning forward. Second, they drive us to harmonize our "system" of designers, developers, product managers, quality assurance engineers, marketers, and others in a transparent, cross-functional collaboration that brings nondesigners into our design process. Last, and perhaps most important, is the mindset shift we gain from adopting a model based on experimentation. Instead of relying on a hero designer to divine the best solution from a single point of view, we use rapid experimentation and measurement to learn quickly how well (or not) our ideas meet our goals. In all of this, the designer's role begins to evolve toward design facilitation, and with that we take on a new set of responsibilities.

Besides Lean Startup, Lean UX has two other foundations: design thinking and Agile development philosophies. Design thinking takes a solution-focused approach to problem solving, working collaboratively to iterate an endless, shifting path toward perfection. It works toward product goals via specific ideation, prototyping, implementation, and learning steps to bring the appropriate solution to light. Agile refocuses software development on value. It seeks to deliver working software to customers quickly and to adjust regularly to new learning along the way.

Lean UX uses these foundations to break the stalemate between the speed of Agile and the need for design in the product-development lifecycle. If you've struggled to figure our how UX design can work in Agile environments, Lean UX can help.

Lean UX breaks down the barriers that have kept software designers isolated from real business needs on the one hand and actual implementation on the other. Lean UX not only brings software designers to the table but also brings our partners in business and technology to the whiteboard to work with us on the best solutions in an ongoing way.

I once had a large pharmaceutical client who hired the agency for which I worked to redesign its ecommerce platform with the goal of increasing revenues by 15 percent. I was the lead interaction designer on our team. In the vacuum of our office, we spent months researching the current system, supply chain, competitors, target audience, and contextual-use scenarios. We researched personas and assembled strategic models. I designed a new information architecture for the product catalog and crafted a brand-new shopping and checkout experience.

The project took months. When the work was complete, we packaged it all up into a PowerPoint deck. This was a formidable deck—it would have to be, considering the $600,000 price tag! We went over to the client's office and spent an entire eight-hour day going over each and every pixel and word in that deck. When it was over, the client clapped (really). They loved it. We were relieved. And we never looked at that deck again.

Six months after that meeting, nothing had changed on the client's site. I don't think they ever looked at that deck again, either.

The moral of this story: building a pixel-perfect spec might be a route to raking in six-figure consulting fees, but it's not a way to make a meaningful difference to a real product that is crucial to real users. It's also not the reason that any designer got into the product design business. We got in to build valuable products and services, not to write specs.

Some teams I work with today create entirely new products or services. They are not working within an existing product framework or structure. In "green-field" projects like these, we are simultaneously trying to discover how this new product or service will be used, how it will behave, and how we are going to build it. It's an environment of continual change, and there isn't a lot of time or patience for planning or up-front design.

Other teams work with established products that were created with traditional design and development methods. Their challenge is different. They need to build upon existing platforms while increasing revenue and brand value. These teams usually have more resources at their disposal than a ground-floor startup, but they still have to use their resources efficiently to build products and services their customers actually want.

As I've learned to practice Lean UX, I've had to overcome the feeling that I was showing work that was "ugly," "unfinished," or "not ready." Working this way requires the support of a high-functioning team. You need to know—as a team—that you're not going to get it right the first time and that you're all working together to iterate your way forward. I want you to gain that confidence, too. Within the pages of this book, I've distilled the insights and tactics that have allowed me to create real success for product and business teams, and real satisfaction for customers.

Who Is Lean UX For?

This book is for interaction designers who know they can contribute more and be more effective with their teams. It's also for product managers who need better ways to define their products with their teams and to validate them with their customers. It's also for developers who understand that a collaborative team environment leads to better code and more meaningful work. And finally, it's for managers—managers of user-experience teams, project teams, business lines, departments, and companies—who understand the difference a great user experience can make.

What's In It for You?

The book is set up in three sections.

- Section I provides an overview and introduction to Lean UX and its founding principles. I lay out the reasons that the evolution of the UX design process is so critical and describe what Lean UX is. I also discuss the underlying principles you'll need to understand to make Lean UX successful.

- Section II focuses on process. Each chapter takes a step in the Lean UX cycle and details clearly how to do each step and why it's important. I also share examples of how I and others have done these things in the past.

- Section III tackles the integration of Lean UX practices into your organization. I discuss the role of Lean UX within a typical Agile development environment. I also discuss the organizational shifts that need to take place at the corporate level, the team level, and at the individual contributor level for these ideas to truly take hold.

My hope is that this book will deliver a wake-up call to user experience designers still waiting for Phase II. Although the book is filled with tactics and techniques to help evolve your processes, I'd like you to remember that Lean UX is, at its core, a mindset.

A Note from Jeff

There are many folks who have been patient, supportive, and inspirational in the writing of this book. Josh and I wanted to take a moment to thank them.

First, I'd like to acknowledge Eric Ries for driving the Lean Startup movement and urging me to write this book. His support came in various forms, including perspectives on design's role in Lean Startup and experience with the book-writing process. He served as a proverbial shoulder to cry on, on more than one occasion.

Next, I'd like to thank Mary Treseler, my editor at O'Reilly. We've spent many hours on emails, phone calls, and the occasional in-person meeting working through editorial strategies, writing tactics, and reviews to arrive—triumphantly, I might add—at the book we have today. Thank you.

Along the way, I teamed up with Matthew Rothenberg to get over the hump of midcycle reviews. His camaraderie, humor, wit, and editorial guidance helped shape the final version of the book and added a much-needed humanity to the words.

I'd like to thank my writing partner Josh Seiden. We spent a lot of time working, teaching, traveling, and hanging out together in 2012, so it only made logical sense for him to join the project and help bring it to the finish line. The book wouldn't be what it is today without his insight and tough-love editing style. I'm a better writer for it and this is a better book because of him. Thanks, Josh.

I would particularly like to thank the many folks who have contributed material to the book. By the end of the project, we had more case studies and contributions than we could use, so some of the wonderful material our colleagues shared didn't fit into the manuscript. This issue reflects more on our writing process than the quality of the contribution. With that said, thanks to Stuart Eccles, Ian Collingwood, Lane Halley, James O'Brien, Adam Silver, Antoine Veliz, Anders Ramsay, Desiree Sy, Zach Larson, Emily Holmes, Greg Petroff, and Duane Bray.

Many of the teams I've worked with over the years inspired the ideas covered in the book. We learned them together and helped build better products together—as well as happier and more productive teams. I know you'll see your influence in the case studies, stories, and anecdotes in these pages.

Finally, I want to acknowledge the love, patience, and support I've had from my family over the 18 months it took to reach a final manuscript. My wife Carrie has dealt with far too many hours of me locked in my office tapping at the keyboard. That sacrifice is not lost on me. My daughters Grace and Sophie have also watched their dad huddled in front of his laptop far too much. I'm sure they're looking forward to having me back in their life. I love you guys. Thank you.

A Note from Josh

In this book, Jeff and I describe a working style that is deeply collaborative. That's my preferred style of working—I always feel that I learn more and am more effective when I'm collaborating. Whatever I've been able to contribute to this book is a result of the amazing collaborations I've been lucky enough to enjoy in my career.

There are a few folks I'd like to single out, though. Alan Cooper first taught me what it means to design software. Working with Alan, I met Jeanine Harriman, who (many years later) first opened my eyes to many of the informal, collaborative techniques we describe in this book. Janice Fraser introduced me to Lean Startup and gave me an opportunity to explore these techniques at LUXr (the Lean UX Residency). Lauralee Alben gave me the courage to open a studio to pursue these ideas, and Giff Constable gave me the kick in the ass to actually open that studio. My friends in the Balanced Team (*http://www.balancedteam.org*) group have had a deep influence on my thinking.

Special thanks go to Lane Halley, who is one of the most gifted practitioners I've ever met and a dear friend. Whenever I am confused, I ask myself, "What would Lane do?" and I usually find a way forward.

I want to thank Jeff for inviting me to join him in bringing this book to market. The book is in his voice because this is his story. It's also been his baby, his passion, and his burden for a long time, so I'm grateful he opened the door for me to join him. I'm continually impressed by his ability to collaborate with grace. Jeff and I have spent a lot of time working together this year, and I'm very proud of that collaboration.

Thanks, finally, to Vicky, Naomi, and Amanda. I love you.

From Jeff and Josh

This book is our attempt to capture what we know about Lean UX at this moment. Lean methods are learning methods, and we expect to be learning and discovering more as we continue our journey. As you travel down this path, we'd love to hear about your journey—your successes, challenges, and failures—so that we can keep learning through our collaboration with you. Please keep in touch with us and share your thoughts. You can reach us at *jeff@jeffgothelf.com* and *josh@joshuaseiden.com*. We look forward to hearing from you.

INTRODUCTION AND PRINCIPLES

In this first section, I provide an introduction to Lean UX and its founding principles. I discuss why the evolution of the UX design process is so critical and describe what Lean UX is. I also discuss the underlying principles you'll need to understand to make Lean UX successful.

Chapter 1, "Why Lean UX?" provides a brief history of UX design and why the time is right for the evolution of that design process.

In Chapter 2, "Principles," I present a detailed look at the key principles that drive the Lean UX process. These principles offer a framework for a leaner product-design process and also provide basic management guidelines for product-design teams. They are critical to the success of Lean UX and, if incorporated into your organization, will have profound impact on your culture and on the productivity and success of your teams.

Why Lean UX?

When bringing our craft to software in the 1980s and 1990s, designers approached software in the same way we approached the earlier materials we worked with. In industrial design, print design, fashion design, and any field involving physical outputs, the manufacturing step is a critical constraint. When designing for physical materials, designers need to figure out what we're making before we start production, because production is expensive. It's expensive to set up a factory floor to produce hard goods or garments. It's expensive to set up a printing press for a print run.

Working in software, designers faced new challenges. We had to figure out the grammar of this new medium, and as we did, we saw new specialties such as interaction design and information architecture emerge. But the process by which designers practiced remained largely unchanged. We still designed products in great detail in advance, because we still had to deal with a "manufacturing" process: our work had to be duplicated onto floppy disks and CDs, which were then distributed to market in exactly the same way that physical goods were distributed. The cost of getting it wrong remained high.

Today, we face a new reality. The Internet has changed the distribution of software in radical ways. Most software is now distributed online. We are no longer limited by a physical manufacturing process and are free to work in much shorter release cycles.

But "free" really undersells this new reality. Teams are now facing intense pressure from competitors who are using techniques such as agile software development, continuous integration, and continuous deployment to radically reduce their cycle times. Teams are pushing new code to production as fast as you can save a Photoshop file. And they are using these short cycles as a competitive advantage—releasing early and often, gaining market feedback, and iterating based on what they learn—and (perhaps inadvertently) raising customer expectations in terms of quality and response times.

In this new reality, traditional "get it all figured out first" approaches are not workable. So what should designers do?

It's time for a change. *Lean UX* (UX = user experience) is the evolution of product design. It takes the best parts of the designer's tool kit and recombines them in a way that makes them relevant to this new reality.

Lean UX is deeply collaborative and cross-functional, because we no longer have the luxury of working in isolation from the rest of the product team. We can't continue to ask our teams to wait for us to figure it all out. We need daily, continuous engagement with our teams if we are going to be effective. This continuous engagement allows us to strip away heavy deliverables in favor of techniques that allow us to build *shared understanding* with our teammates.

Lean UX also lets us change the way we talk about design. Instead of talking about features and documents, we can talk about what works. In this new reality, we have more access to market feedback than ever before. This feedback allows us to reframe design conversations in terms of objective business goals. We can measure what works, learn, and adjust.

Lean UX is three things. It's easiest to understand as a process change for designers. But it's more than that. It's a mindset that lets us approach our work in new ways. It's also a way of thinking about managing software. I'll dig into each one of these concepts throughout the book. In the next chapter we'll take a look at the principles that lay the foundation for Lean UX design.

Principles

At the heart of Lean UX, you'll find a core set of principles. These principles cover process, collaboration, management, and more. Teams guided by all these principles will get the most out of the Lean UX approach. Start with these principles to get your teams pointed in the right direction, and keep them in mind as you start to implement the Lean UX processes I describe later in this book. You will inevitably have to adjust the Lean UX processes to fit them into your organization, and the principles explained in this chapter will provide guidance to you for that work.

Ultimately, if you're able to put these principles to work, you'll find that you will change your organization's culture. Some will have more impact than others and will be more difficult to push through. Others will be easier to act on. Regardless, each principle detailed here will help you build a product design organization that is more collaborative, more cross-functional, and a more useful fit for today's reality.

The Three Foundations of Lean UX

Lean UX stands on three foundations. The first foundation is *design thinking*.

Tim Brown, CEO and president of legendary design firm IDEO, described design thinking as "innovation powered by...direct observation of what people want and need in their lives and what they like or dislike about the way particular products are made, packaged, marketed, sold, and supported...[It's] a discipline that uses the designer's sensibility and methods to match people's needs with what is technologically feasible and what a viable business strategy can convert into customer value and market opportunity."[1]

Design thinking is important for Lean UX because it takes the explicit position that every aspect of a business can be approached with design methods. It gives designers permission and precedent to work beyond their typical boundaries. It also encourages nondesigners to use design methods to solve the problems they face in their roles. Design thinking is a critical foundation that encourages teams to collaborate across roles and consider product design from a holistic perspective.

The second foundation of Lean UX is *Agile software development*. Software developers have been using Agile methods for years to reduce their cycle times and deliver customer value in a continuous manner. Although Agile methods can pose process challenges for designers (solutions are provided in Section III), the core values of Agile are at the heart of Lean UX. Lean UX applies the four core principles of Agile development to product design:

1. **Individuals and interactions over processes and tools.** To generate the best solutions quickly, you must engage the entire team. Ideas must be exchanged freely and frequently. The constraints of current processes and production tools are eschewed in favor of conversation with colleagues.

2. **Working software over comprehensive documentation.** Every business problem has endless solutions, and each member of a team will have an opinion on which is best. The challenge is figuring out which solution is most viable. By building working software sooner, solutions can be assessed for market fit and viability.

3. **Customer collaboration over contract negotiation.** Collaborating with your teammates and customers builds a shared understanding of the problem space and proposed solutions. It creates consensus behind decisions. The result? Faster iterations, real involvement in product making, and team investment in validated learning. It also lessens dependency on heavy documentation, as everyone on the team has already participated in making the decisions that were used to require written communication and defense.

4. **Responding to change over following a plan.** The assumption in Lean UX is that the initial product designs will be wrong, so the goal should be to find out what's wrong with them as soon as possible. Once we discover what's working and what's not, we adjust our proposals and test again. This input from the market keeps us agile, constantly nudging us in a "more right" direction.

---

1   *http://hbr.org/2008/06/design-thinking/ar/1*

The third foundation of Lean UX is the *Lean Startup method* founded by Eric Ries. Lean Startup uses a feedback loop called "build-measure-learn" to minimize project risk and gets teams building quickly and learning quickly. Teams build *Minimum Viable Products* (MVPs) and ship them quickly to begin the process of learning as early as possible.

As Eric puts it, "Lean Startup initially advocates the creation of rapid prototypes designed to test market assumptions and uses customer feedback to evolve them much faster than more traditional software engineering practices...Lean Startup processes reduce waste by increasing the frequency of contact with real customers, therefore testing and avoiding incorrect market assumptions as early as possible."[2] Lean UX is a direct application of this philosophy to the practice of product design.

Each design is a proposed business solution—a hypothesis. Your goal is to validate the proposed solution as efficiently as possible by using customer feedback. The smallest thing you can build to test each hypothesis is your MVP. The MVP doesn't have to be made of code; it can be an approximation of the end experience. You collect what you learn from your MVP and then evolve your ideas. Then you do it again.

The practice of Lean UX is: *Lean UX is the practice of bringing the true nature of a product to light faster, in a collaborative, cross-functional way that reduces the emphasis on thorough documentation while increasing the focus on building a shared understanding of the actual product experience being designed.*

Principles

In the rest of this chapter, I'll lay out the principles behind Lean UX. As you explore the Lean UX approach, keep these principles in mind. Think of your experience with Lean UX as a learning journey. Use these principles to keep you and your team on course.

Principle: Cross-Functional Teams

What is it? Cross-functional teams are made up of the various disciplines involved in creating your product. Software engineering, product management, interaction design, visual design, content strategy, marketing, and quality assurance (QA) should all be included in a Lean UX team. Lean UX demands a high level of collaboration between these disciplines. Their involvement must be continuous, from day one of the project until the end of the engagement.

---

2   *The Lean Startup* (Crown Business, 2011).

Why do it? The creation of these diverse teams collapses the gated-handoff process known as *waterfall*. Insight on each idea is brought in from all relevant disciplines earlier in the process. Conversation is encouraged across functional silos, which drives greater team efficiency.

Principle: Small, Dedicated, Colocated

What is it? Keep your teams small—no more than 10 total core people. Dedicate them to one project and staff it all out of the same location.

Why do it? The benefit of small teams comes down to three words: communication, focus, and camaraderie. Smaller teams are easier to keep current on project status, changes, and new learning. Dedicating your team to one project keeps everyone on the team focused on the same priorities all the time. Having the team all in one place allows relationships to grow between colleagues.

Principle: Progress = Outcomes, Not Output

What is it? Features and services are *outputs*. The business goals they are meant to achieve are *outcomes*. Lean UX measures progress in terms of explicitly defined business outcomes.

Why do it? When we attempt to predict which features will achieve specific outcomes, we are mostly engaging in speculation. Although it's easier to manage toward the launch of specific feature sets, we don't know in any meaningful way whether a feature is effective until it's in the market. By managing to outcomes (and the progress made toward them), we gain insight into the efficacy of the features we are building. If a feature is not performing well, we can make an objective decision as to whether it should be kept, changed, or replaced.

Principle: Problem-Focused Teams

What is it? A problem-focused team is one that has been assigned a business problem to solve, as opposed to a set of features to implement. This is the logical extension of the focus on outcomes.

Why do it? Assigning teams problems to solve shows trust in those teams. It allows them to come up with their own solutions and drives a deeper sense of pride and ownership in the solutions the team implements.

Principle: Removing Waste

What is it? One of the core tenets in Lean manufacturing is the removal of anything that doesn't lead to the ultimate goal. In Lean UX, the ultimate goal is improved outcomes; hence, anything that doesn't contribute to that is considered waste and should be removed from the team's process.

Why do it? Team resources are limited. The more waste the team can eliminate, the faster they can move. Teams want to work on the right challenges. They want to be effective. A discipline of waste removal can help teams keep their laser focus where it belongs.

Principle: Small Batch Size

What is it? Another fundamental from Lean manufacturing is the use of small batch sizes. Lean manufacturing uses this notion to keep inventory low and quality high. Translated to Lean UX, this concept means creating only the design that is necessary to move the team forward and avoiding a big "inventory" of untested and unimplemented design ideas.

Why do it? Large-batch design makes the team less efficient. It forces the team to wait for big design deliverables. It keeps the team from learning whether their ideas are valid. It keeps some teammates idle and inevitably results in design assets that go unused. This approach is wasteful and doesn't maximize the full learning potential of the team.

Principle: Continuous Discovery

What is it? Continuous discovery is the ongoing process of engaging the customer during the design and development process. This engagement is done through regularly scheduled activities, using both quantitative and qualitative methods. The goal is to understand what the users are doing with your products and why they are doing it. Research is done on frequent and regular schedules. Research involves the entire team.

Why do it? Regular customer conversations provide frequent opportunities for validating new product ideas. By bringing the entire team into the research cycle, the team will develop empathy for users and the problems they face. Finally, as the team learns together, you reduce the need for future debrief conversations and documentation.

Principle: GOOB: The New User-Centricity

What is it? It may sound like a baby's first word, but GOOB is actually an acronym for what Stanford professor, entrepreneur, and author Steve Blank calls "getting out of the building." It's the realization that meeting-room debates about user needs won't be settled conclusively within your office. Instead, the answers lie out in the marketplace, outside of your building.

After years of advocating for customer research, the UX community has a champion from the business world in Steve Blank. Blank's prescription: give potential customers a chance to provide feedback on your ideas sooner than you would have in the past. Much sooner. Test your ideas with a strong dose of reality while they're still young. Better to find out that your ideas are missing the mark before you've spent time and resources building a product that no one wants.

Why do it? Ultimately, the success or failure of your product isn't the team's decision—it's the customers'. They will have to click that "Buy Now" button you designed. The sooner you give them a voice, the sooner you'll learn whether you've got an idea that's ready to be built.

Principle: Shared Understanding

What is it? Shared understanding is the collective knowledge of the team that builds up over time as the team works together. It's a rich understanding of the space, the product, and the customers.

Why do it? Shared understanding is the currency of Lean UX. The more a team collectively understands what it's doing and why, the less it has to depend on secondhand reports and detailed documents to continue its work.

Principle: Anti-Pattern: Rockstars, Gurus, and Ninjas

What is it? Lean UX advocates a team-based mentality. Rockstars, gurus, ninjas, and other elite experts of their craft break down team cohesion and eschew collaboration.

Why do it? Rockstars don't share—neither their ideas nor the spotlight. Team cohesion breaks down when you add individuals with large egos who are determined to stand out and be stars. When collaboration breaks down, you lose the environment you need to create the shared understanding that allows you [to avoid repetition] to move forward effectively.

Principle: Externalizing Your Work

What is it? Externalizing means getting your work out of your head and out of your computer and into public view. Teams use whiteboards, foam-core boards, artifact walls, printouts, and sticky notes to expose their work in progress to their teammates, colleagues, and customers.

Why do it? Externalizing gets ideas out of teammates' heads and on to the wall, allowing everyone to see where the team stands. It creates a passive, ambient flow of information across the team. It inspires new ideas that build off the ones that have already been shared. It allows all the members of the team—even the quiet ones—to participate in information-sharing activities. Their sticky notes or whiteboard sketches are equally as loud as those of the most prominent person on the team.

Principle: Making over Analysis

What is it? Lean UX values making over analysis. There is more value in creating the first version of an idea than spending half a day debating its merits in a conference room.

Why do it? The answer to most difficult questions the team will face will not be answered in a conference room. Instead, they will be answered by customers in the field. In order to get those answers, you need to make the ideas concrete—you need to make something for people to respond to. Debating ideas is waste. Instead of analyzing potential scenarios, make something and get out of the building with it.

Principle: Learning over Growth

What is it? It's difficult to figure out the right thing to build and scale a business around that thing at the same time. They are contradictory activities. Lean UX favors a focus on learning first and scaling second.

Why do it? Scaling an idea that is unproven is risky. It might work. And it might not. If it doesn't work and you've scaled it out to your entire user base, your team has wasted valuable time and resources. Ensuring that an idea is right before scaling it out mitigates the risk inherent in broad feature deployment.

Principle: Permission to Fail

What is it? In order to find the best solution to business problems, Lean UX teams need to experiment with ideas. Most of these ideas will fail. The team must be safe to fail if they are to be successful. *Permission to fail* means that the team has a safe environment in which to experiment. That philosophy applies to both the technical environment (they can push out ideas in a safe way) and the cultural environment (they won't be penalized for trying ideas that don't succeed).

Why do it? Permission to fail breeds a culture of experimentation. Experimentation breeds creativity. Creativity, in turn, yields innovative solutions. When teams don't fear for their jobs if they get something wrong, they're more apt to take risks. It is from those risks that big ideas ultimately come. Finally, as the following anecdote illustrates so beautifully, frequent failures lead to increased mastery of skills.

In a video called "Why You Need to Fail" (*http://www.youtube.com/ watch?v=HhxcFGuKOys*), CD Baby founder Derek Sivers describes the surprising results of a ceramics class. On the first day, the instructor announced to his class that the students would be divided into two groups. Half of the students would need to make only one clay pot each during the semester. Their grades would depend on the perfection of that solitary pot. The other half of the class would be graded simply by the weight of the pots they made during the semester. If they made 50 pounds of pots or more, they'd get an A. Forty pounds would earn a B; 30 pounds, a C; and so on. What they actually made was irrelevant. The instructor said he wouldn't even look at their pots. He would bring his bathroom scale to the final day of class and weigh the students' work.

At the end of the semester, an interesting thing had occurred. Outside observers of the class noted that the highest-quality pots had been made by the "quantity group." They had spent the entire semester working as quickly as they could to make pots. Sometimes they succeeded, and sometimes they failed. With each iteration, each experiment, they learned. From that learning, they became better able to achieve the end goal: making high-quality clay pots.

By contrast, the group that made one object didn't have the benefit of those failed iterations and didn't learn quickly enough to perform at the same level as the "quantity group." They had spent their semester theorizing about what would make a "grade-A" clay pot but didn't have the experience to execute that grandiose vision.

Principle: Getting Out of the Deliverables Business

What is it? Lean UX refocuses the design process away from the documents the team is creating to the outcomes the team is achieving. With increased cross-functional collaboration, stakeholder conversation becomes less about what artifact is being created and more about which outcome is being achieved.

Why do it? Documents don't solve customer problems—good products do. The team's focus should be on learning which features have the biggest impact on the their customers. The artifacts the team uses to gain that knowledge are irrelevant. All that matters is the quality of the product, as measured by the market's reaction to it.

Wrapping Up: Principles

This chapter put forward a set of foundational principles for Lean UX. These are the core attributes that any Lean UX team must embody. As you begin to form your Lean UX practice, I encourage you to use these principles to define your team's makeup, location, goals, and practices.

In Section II, I'll put these principles into action as I detail the entire Lean UX process.

PROCESS

It's Tuesday and Rick, Mark, Olga, and Arti are standing at the whiteboard, looking at a wireframe that they've drawn. Arti has a marker in her hand, but she's not drawing. "Rick, I don't understand what you're driving at. Can you explain the problem?"

Rick takes the marker, wipes clear a section of the board, and explains the regulation again. The team is designing an app for stock traders, and the app has to obey a strict set of regulations. Rick, the business analyst, is responsible for making sure that the team's designs support the rules.

After a while, the team is nodding, and Arti takes the marker again. She suggests a change to the wireframe design of the app on the board and the team nods again. They all take out their iPhones, take photos of the board, and agree to reconvene the next day. They're confident that what they've agreed on will be ready for user testing on Thursday.

Arti, the designer, goes back to her desk to start detailing the design they've sketched. Mark, the front-end developer, starts building the page—he uses premade components from the living style guide the team has put in place, so he doesn't need to wait for Arti before getting the basic pieces in place. Rick opens the project's wiki and begins to document the decisions the team has made about the application behavior. He'll review these choices with the product owner later in the day. And Olga, the QA tester, begins the process of writing tests for the new section of the app.

This is the day-to-day rhythm of Lean UX: a team working collaboratively, iteratively, and in parallel, with few handoffs, minimal deliverables, and a focus on working software and market feedback. In this section, you'll see how it's done.

In the previous section, I showed you the ideas behind Lean UX—the principles that drive the work. In this section, I get very practical and describe in detail the process of implementing Lean UX.

Chapter 3, "Vision, Framing, and Outcomes," describes how Lean UX radically shifts the way we frame our work. Our goal is not to create a deliverable, it's to change something in the world—to create an outcome. In this chapter I'll describe the key tool we use to do this: hypothesis statements.

Chapter 4, "Collaborative Design," describes the shift in our design process. Lean UX uses many techniques familiar to designers but shifts the emphasis of our work. We become more collaborative. We aim for speed first. We prioritize learning. We use a key tool to achieve this: the MVP.

Chapter 5, "MVPs and Experiments," is about experiments. Lean UX is based on the idea that we begin our work with an assumption. We use experiments to test our assumptions and then build on what we learn in those experiments. This chapter shows you how to orient your design process around experiments and learning.

Chapter 6, "Feedback and Research," deals with feedback. User Experience work in any form requires good input from users. Lean UX puts a premium on continuous feedback to help us guide our design process. This chapter shows you techniques that Lean UX teams use to get feedback early and often, and how to incorporate that feedback into future product iterations.

CHAPTER 3

Vision, Framing, and Outcomes

If it disagrees with experiment, it's wrong.

Dr. Richard Feynman

Traditionally, UX design projects are framed by requirements and deliverables; teams are given requirements and expected to produce deliverables. Lean UX radically shifts the way we frame our work. Our goal is not to create a deliverable, it's to change something in the world—to create an outcome. We start with assumptions instead of requirements. We create and test hypotheses. We measure to see whether we've achieved our desired outcomes.

This chapter covers the main tool of outcome-focused work: the hypothesis statement. The hypothesis statement is the starting point for a project. It states a clear vision for the work and shifts the conversation between team members and their managers from outputs (e.g., "we will create a single sign-on feature") to outcomes (e.g., "we want to increase the number of new sign-ups to our service").

The hypothesis statement is a way of expressing assumptions in testable form. It is composed of the following elements:

Assumptions

A high-level declaration of what we believe to be true.

Hypotheses

More granular descriptions of our assumptions that target specific areas of our product or workflow for experimentation.

Outcomes

The signal we seek from the market to help us validate or invalidate our hypotheses. These are often quantitative but can also be qualitative.

Personas

Models of the people for whom we believe we are solving a problem.

Features

The product changes or improvements we believe will drive the outcomes we seek.

Let's take a look at each one of these elements in further detail.

Assumptions

The first step in the Lean UX process is to declare your assumptions. Every project starts with assumptions, but usually we don't explicitly acknowledge this fact. Instead, we try to ignore assumptions, or worse, treat them as facts.

Declaring your assumptions allows your team to create a common starting point. By doing this as a team, you give every team member—designer and nondesigner alike—the opportunity to voice his or her opinion on how best to solve the problem. Going through an assumptions declaration exercise gets everyone's ideas out on the whiteboard. It reveals the team's divergence of opinions and also exposes a broad set of possible solutions.

Declaring assumptions is the first step in the Lean UX process; see Figure 3-1.

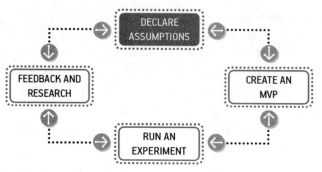

Figure 3-1. *The Lean UX process, step 1*

Method: Declaring Assumptions

Who

Declaring assumptions is a group exercise. Gather your team, making sure that all disciplines are represented, including any subject matter experts that could have vital knowledge about your project. For example, if you're handling a frequent customer complaint, it might be beneficial to include a customer service representative from your call center. Call center reps speak to more customers than anyone else in the organization, and will likely have insight the rest of the team won't.

Preparation

Give the team advance notice of the problem they will be taking on to give everyone a chance to prepare any material they need, or do any related research, before you begin. Important things to prepare in advance include:

1. Analytics reports that show how the current product is being used

2. Usability reports that illustrate why customers are taking certain actions in your product

3. Information about past attempts to fix this issue and their successes and failures

4. Analysis from the business stakeholder as to how solving this problem will affect the company's performance

5. Competitive analyses that show how competitors are tackling the same issues

Method: Problem Statement

The team needs to have a starting point for the exercise. I've found it helpful to start with a problem statement. (See the template for this statement later in this section.) The problem statement gives your team a clear focus for their work. It also defines any important constraints. You need constraints for group work. They provide the guardrails that keep the team grounded and aligned.

Problem statement template

Problem statements are made up of three elements:

1. The current goals of the product or system

2. The problem the business stakeholder wants addressed (i.e., where the goals aren't being met)

3. An explicit request for improvement that doesn't dictate a specific solution

   Template

   [Our service/product] *was designed to achieve* **[these goals]**. *We have observed that the product/service isn't meeting* **[these goals]**, *which is causing* **[this adverse effect]** *to our business. How might we improve* **[service/product]** *so that our customers are more successful based on* **[these measurable criteria]**?

For example, here is a problem statement we used to begin a project at TheLadders, an online recruiting firm where I worked. (You'll see many more examples from TheLadders throughout this book.)

> *Our service offers a conduit between job seekers and employers trying to hire them. Through our service, employers can reach out to job seekers in our ecosystem with employment opportunities. We have observed that one critical factor affecting customer satisfaction is how frequently job seekers respond to employer messages. Currently, job seekers are replying to these communications at a very low rate. How might we improve the efficacy of our communication products, thus making employers more successful in their jobs and job seekers more satisfied with our service?*

Problem statements are filled with assumptions. The team's job is to dissect the problem statement into its core assumptions. You can do that by using the following business assumptions worksheet. Note that some teams—especially teams starting from scratch—may not have a clear problem statement. That's okay. You can still try out the worksheet. You'll just have to expect that it may take longer to reach consensus on some of the questions.

Business Assumptions Worksheet

I like to use this worksheet (created by my partner Giff Constable) to facilitate the assumptions discussion. There are many ways to complete this worksheet. You can answer the questions as a team, simply discussing each answer. Or you can run a structured brainstorm/affinity mapping exercise for each question. However you do it, remember that it's important to give everyone a chance to contribute. Also, don't worry if you get to the end of the worksheet without clear agreement on all of the answers. The goal is to collect statements that reflect what you and your team think might be true. If you have strong disagreement on a point, capture the different perspectives.

Assumptions Worksheet

Business Assumptions

1. I believe my customers have a need to _____.
2. These needs can be solved with _____.
3. My initial customers are (or will be) _____.
4. The #1 value a customer wants to get out of my service is _____.
5. The customer can also get these additional benefits _____.
6. I will acquire the majority of my customers through _____.
7. I will make money by _____.
8. My primary competition in the market will be _____.
9. We will beat them due to _____.
10. My biggest product risk is _____.
11. We will solve this through _____.
12. What other assumptions do we have that, if proven false, will cause our business/project to fail? _____.

User Assumptions

1. Who is the user?
2. Where does our product fit in his work or life?
3. What problems does our product solve?
4. When and how is our product used?
5. What features are important?
6. How should our product look and behave?

You may discover that some of these questions don't apply to your project. That's okay—you can adapt the questions to your situation as you see fit. If it's early in the life of your product, you'll probably spend more time on the business assumptions. If you've got a mature product, you'll probably focus your energies on the user assumptions. The point is to cast a broad net and look for assumptions in all dimensions of your project.

When you've completed the worksheet, you will have a list of assumption statements. Your next step is to prioritize these assumptions.

Prioritizing assumptions

The reason we declare assumptions at the start of our work is so that we can identify project risks. Once you have a list of assumptions, you need to figure out which ones are the riskiest so that you can work on them first.

Lean UX is an exercise in ruthless prioritization. Understanding that you can't test every assumption, how do you decide which one to test first? I like to create a chart like the one in Figure 3-2, and use it to map out the list of assumptions.

The goal is to prioritize a set of assumptions to test based on their level of risk (i.e., how bad would it be if we were wrong about this?) and how much understanding we have of the issue. The higher the risk and the more unknowns involved, the higher the priority to test those assumptions.

This doesn't mean that assumptions that don't make the first cut are gone forever. Keep a backlog of the other assumptions you've identified so you can come back to them and test them if and when it makes sense to do so.

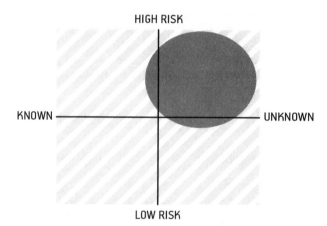

Figure 3-2. *Prioritization matrix*

Hypotheses

With your prioritized list of assumptions in hand, you're ready to move to the next step: testing your assumptions. To do that, transform each assumption statement into a format that is easier to test: a hypothesis statement.

Generally, hypothesis statements use the format:

> *We believe* [this statement is true].

> *We will know we're* [right/wrong] *when we see the following feedback from the market:*

[qualitative feedback] *and/or* [quantitative feedback] *and/or* [key performance indicator change].

You can see that this format has two parts. A statement of what you believe to be true, and a statement of the market feedback you're looking for to confirm that you're right.

Expressing your assumptions this way turns out to be a really powerful technique. It takes much of the subjective and political conversation out of the decision-making process and instead orients the team toward feedback from the market. It also orients the team toward users and customers.

Subhypotheses: Breaking the Hypothesis Down into Smaller Parts

Sometimes—if not most of the time—you will discover that your hypothesis is too big to test with one test. It will contain too many moving parts, too many subhypotheses. When this happens, I find it helpful to break the hypothesis down into smaller and more specific parts. Though there are many ways to do this, for product work I have found that this format is very helpful:

We believe that

[doing this/building this feature/creating this experience]

for [these people/personas]

will achieve [this outcome].

We will know this is true when we see

[this market feedback, quantitative measure, or qualitative insight].

The first field is completed with the feature or improvement you're considering making to your product. The second field describes exactly which of your target customers will benefit from this feature. The last field speaks to the benefit those customers will get from that feature. The final statement ties it all together. This is the statement that determines whether your hypothesis was true. What market feedback will you look for to indicate that your idea is correct? This feedback could be a quantitatively measured usage of a feature, an increase in a business metric, or a qualitative assessment of some sort.

It's not all numbers! It's worth noting that there's been a lot of backlash in the design world against measurement-driven design. The argument is that by reducing every design decision to factors that can be measured, we take the delight and soul out of our products. I actually agree with this perspective, which is why I think it's so important to include qualitative feedback in your success criteria. Are people delighted by a design? Do they recommend your product to their friends? Do they tweet about it? When you look for success metrics, remember that it's not all numbers.

Let's take a look at an example of how this works by going back to the problem statement we looked at earlier from TheLadders:

> *Our service offers a conduit between job seekers and employers trying to hire them. Through our service, employers can reach out to job seekers in our ecosystem with employment opportunities. We have observed that one critical factor affecting customer satisfaction is how frequently job seekers respond to employer messages. Currently, job seekers are replying to these communications at a very low rate. How can we improve the efficacy of our communication products, thus making employers more successful in their jobs and job seekers more satisfied with our service?*

One assumption we make in this problem statement is that recruiters will use a new channel (TheLadders) to engage with candidates. This is not a proven fact and needs to be tested. How would we write the hypothesis for that statement? Let's take our template and fill it out:

> *We believe that*
>
> *creating an efficient communication system within TheLadders' product experience*
>
> *for recruiters and employers*
>
> *will achieve a higher rate of contact success and an increase in product satisfaction.*
>
> *We will know this is true when we see an increase in the number of replies from job seekers to recruiter contacts and an increase in the number of messages initiated by recruiters in our system.*

Completing Your Hypothesis Statements

To create your hypothesis statements, start assembling the building blocks. Put together a list of *outcomes* you are trying to create, a definition of the *personas* you are trying to service, and a set of the *features* you believe might work in this situation. Once you've got all of this raw material, you can put them all together into a set of statements. Let's take a closer look at each of these elements.

Outcomes

When you're creating hypotheses to test, you want to try to be very specific regarding the outcomes you are trying to achieve. I discussed earlier how Lean UX teams focus less on output (the documents, the drawings, even the products and features that we create) and more on the outcomes that these outputs create: can we make it easier for people to log into our site? Can we encourage more people to sign up? Can we encourage greater collaboration among system users?

Together with your team, look at the problem you are trying to solve. You probably have a few high-level outcomes you are hoping to achieve (e.g., increasing signups, increasing usage, etc.). Consider how you can break down these high-level outcomes into smaller parts. What behaviors will predict greater usage: more visitors to the site? Greater click-through on email marketing? Increasing number of items in the shopping cart? Sometimes it's helpful to run a team brainstorm to create a list of individual outcomes that, taken together, you believe will predict the larger outcome you seek.

Figure 3-3 shows an example from Giff Constable, in which an executive leadership team brainstormed and then voted on which key performance indicators (KPIs) the company should pursue next. After consolidating to the list shown in the photo, each executive was given four M&Ms. As long as they managed not to eat their votes, these executives were able to vote (with candy) for each metric they felt was most important. Ties were broken by the CEO.

Figure 3-3. *KPI prioritization with candy*

Personas

Designers often create models called personas to represent the users of their systems. If your team already has a well-defined set of personas, the only thing you need to consider at this point is which ones you will be using in your hypothesis statements. If you don't yet have personas, this section explains how to create personas for the Lean UX process.

Proto-Personas

Designers have long been advocates for the end user. Lean UX is no different. As we make assumptions about our business and the outcomes we'd like to achieve, we still need to keep the user front and center in our thinking.

Most of us learned to think about personas as a tool to represent what we learned in our research. It was often the case that we created personas as the output of lengthy, expensive research studies. The problem with personas that are created this way is the assumption that this is the only way to create personas, as well as the tendency to regard personas created through this process as untouchable because of all of the work that went into creating them.

In Lean UX, we change the order of operations in the persona process. When creating personas in this approach, we start with assumptions and then do research to validate our assumptions. Instead of spending months in the field interviewing people, we spend a few hours creating *proto-personas*. Proto-personas are our best guess as to who is using (or will use) our product and why. We sketch them on paper with the entire team contributing—we want to capture everyone's assumptions. Then, as we learn from our ongoing research, we quickly find out how accurate our initial guesses are, and how we'll need to adjust our target audience (and persona)—and thus our design.

Using Proto-Personas

A team we were working with in New York was building an app that improved the Community-Supported Agriculture (CSA) experience for New York City residents. CSA is a program that allows city residents to pool their money and purchase an entire season's worth of produce from a local farmer. The farmer then delivers his crops, weekly, to the members of the CSA. Many subscribers to the CSA are men and women in their late twenties and early thirties who need to juggle a busy work life, an active social life, and a desire to participate in the CSA.

The team assumed that most CSA consumers were women who liked to cook. They spent about an hour creating a persona named Susan. But when they went out into the field to do research, they quickly learned that the overwhelming majority of cooks, and hence the potential users of their app, were young men. They returned to the office and revised their persona to create Timothy (Figure 3-4).

Figure 3-4. *Proto-persona example*

Timothy proved to be a far more accurate target user. The team didn't waste any more time refining ideas for the wrong audience. They were now focused on an audience that, while still not perfect, was far more correct than their initial assumptions.

Persona Format

We like to sketch proto-personas on paper using a hand-drawn quadrant, as in Figures 3-5 and 3-6 (start by folding a sheet of paper into four boxes). The top-left quadrant holds a rough sketch of the persona and his or her name and role. The top-right box holds basic demographic information. Try to focus on demographic information that predicts a specific type of behavior. For example, there may be cases in which the persona's age is totally irrelevant yet their access to a specific device, such as an iPhone, will completely change the way they interact with your product.

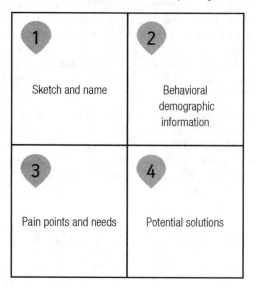

Figure 3-5. *Blank persona template*

The bottom half of the proto-persona is where we put the meat of the information. The bottom-left quadrant contains the user's needs and frustration with the current product or situation, the specific pain points your product is trying to solve, and/or the opportunity you're trying to address. The bottom-right quadrant contains potential solutions for those needs. You'll use the bottom-right quadrant to capture feature and solution ideas.

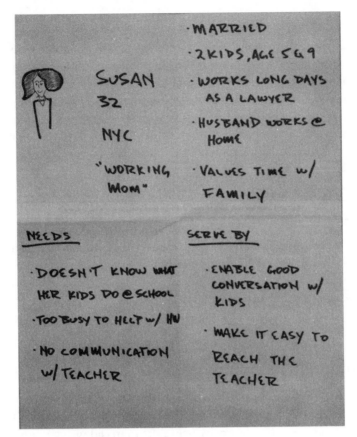

Figure 3-6. *Completed persona template*

Persona Creation Process

As with the other elements of the hypothesis statement, we like to start the persona creation process with a brainstorm. Team members offer up their opinions on who the project should be targeting and how that would affect each potential user's use of the product. Once the brainstorming is complete, the team should narrow down the ideas to an initial set of three or four personas they believe are most likely to be the target audience. Try to differentiate the personas around needs and roles rather than by demographic.

Features

Once you have a list of outcomes in mind and have focused in on a group of users, it's time to start thinking about what tactics, features, products, and services you can put in place to achieve those desired outcomes. Typically, everyone on the team has a strong opinion at this stage—after all, features are the most concrete things we work with, so it's often easiest for us to express our ideas in terms of features. Too often, though, our design process starts when someone has a feature idea, and we end up working backward to try to justify the feature. In Lean UX, features exist to serve the needs of the business, the customer, and the user.

Feature Brainstorming Process

Employing the same techniques described earlier, we like to create feature lists by brainstorming them as a team. We're looking for features we think will drive customer behavior in the desired direction. Have each team member write each idea, using a thick marker, on a sticky note. When time is up, ask everyone to post their notes to the wall and have the group arrange them into themes.

Assembling Your Subhypotheses

With all of your raw material created, you're ready to organize this material into a set of testable hypotheses. We like to create a table like the one in Figure 3-7 and then complete it by using the material we've brainstormed.

As you write your hypotheses, consider which persona(s) you're serving with your proposed solutions. It's not unusual to find solutions that serve more than one persona at a time. It's also not unusual to create a hypothesis in which one feature drives more than one outcome. When you see that happening, split the hypothesis into two parts—you want each statement to refer to only one outcome. The important thing to remember in this whole process is to keep your ideas specific enough so that you can create meaningful tests to see if each of your ideas hold water.

We will	for	In order to achieve
[create this feature]	[this persona]	[this outcome.]

Figure 3-7. *Hypothesis creation table*

When your list of hypotheses is complete, you're ready (finally!) to move on to the next step: design. If you've done the process to this point with your whole team (and I strongly recommend that you do), you'll be in great position to move forward together. This process is a very effective way to create a shared understanding and shared mission across your whole team.

Conclusion

In this chapter, we discussed how we can reframe our work in terms of outcomes, which is is a vitally important Lean UX technique: framing our work with outcomes frees us (and our teams) to search for the best solutions to the problem at hand. We also looked at the process of declaring outcomes. In order to achieve these, we start with the project's problem statements and then acknowledge our assumptions, then transform these assumptions into hypotheses. We also showed how to write hypothesis statements that capture intended features, audience, and goals, and that are specific enough to be tested. You'll end up with statements that will serve as the roadmap for the next step of the Lean UX process: collaborative design.

In the next chapter, we define collaborative design and how it differs from traditional product design. We'll discuss specific tools and techniques that empower teams to design together and demonstrate how designing together is the beginning of the hypothesis validation process.

Collaborative Design

As you navigate through the rest of your life, be open to collaboration. Other people and other people's ideas are often better than your own. Find a group of people who challenge and inspire you, spend a lot of time with them, and it will change your life.

Amy Poehler

Lean UX is a collaborative process. It brings designers and nondesigners together in co-creation. It yields ideas that are bigger and better than those of the individual contributors. But it's not design-by-committee. Instead, Lean UX increases a team's ownership over the work by providing an opportunity for all opinions to be heard much earlier in the process. In this chapter, we explore the many benefits that come from this close, cross-functional collaboration. Specifically, we look at:

- Why everybody gets to design
- How low-fidelity artifacts increase collaboration
- Building a shared understanding across your team

We'll also dig into a series of techniques that enable this more productive way of working, including:

- Design studio—a collaborative sketching exercise for the entire team

- Style guides and pattern libraries—living repositories of all the customer-facing elements of your product

- Collaboration techniques for geographically distributed teams

In the previous chapter, we discussed product feature hypotheses. The first part of a product feature hypothesis statement describes *what* we will build to solve our customers' pain point. These features can be designed in many ways. Navigating through these options can be difficult for teams. How often have you experienced team conflict over design choices?

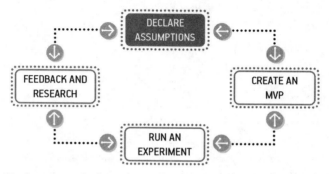

Figure 4-1. *You've written the hypothesis. Now it's time to determine what you'll need to test your assumptions.*

The most effective way I've found to rally a team around a design direction is through collaboration. Over the long haul, collaboration yields better results than hero-based design (the practice of calling in a designer or design team to drop in, come up with something beautiful, and take off to rescue the next project). Teams rarely learn or get better from working with heroes. Instead, designing together increases the design IQ of the entire team. It allows every member of the team to articulate his or her ideas. It gives designers a much broader set of ideas to draw upon as they refine the user experience. This collaboration, in turn, breeds increased feelings of ownership over the work being done by the entire team. Finally, collaborative design builds team-wide shared understanding. It is this shared understanding that is the currency of Lean UX. The more the team collectively understands, the less it has to document in order to move forward.

Collaborative design is an approach that allows a team to create product concepts together. It helps teams build a shared understanding of the design problem and solution. It allows them to work together to decide which functionality and interface elements best implement the feature in their hypothesis.

Collaborative design is still a designer-led activity. It's the designer's responsibility not only to call these meetings but to facilitate them as well. Sometimes you'll have one-on-one sessions with a developer at a whiteboard. Other times, you'll gather the whole team for a Design Studio exercise. The key is to collaborate with a diverse group of team members.

In a typical collaborative design session, teams sketch together, critique the work as it emerges, and ultimately converge on a solution that they feel has the greatest chance of success. The designer, while still producing designs, takes on the additional role of facilitator to lead the team through a series of exercises.

The output of these sessions typically consists of low-fidelity sketches and wireframes. This level of fidelity is critical to maintaining the malleability of the work, which allows the team to pivot quickly if their tests reveal that the approach isn't working. It's much easier to pivot from a failed approach if you haven't spent too much time laboriously documenting and detailing that approach.

Conversation: Your Most Powerful Tool

Lean UX promotes conversation as the primary means of communication among team members. In this way, it is very much in line with the Agile Manifesto, which promotes "individuals and interactions over processes and tools." Conversation unites a team around a shared vision. It also brings insights from different disciplines to the project much earlier than a traditional design cycle would allow. As new ideas are formed or changes are made to the design, a team member's insight can quickly challenge those ideas in a way the designer alone might not have recognized.

By having these conversations early and often, the team is aware of everyone's ideas and can get started on their own work earlier. If they know that the proposed solution requires a certain back-end infrastructure, for example, the team's engineers can get started on that work while the design is refined and finalized. Parallel paths for software development and design are the fastest route to an actual experience.

These conversations may seem awkward at first; after all, you're breaking down time-tested walls between disciplines. As the conversation evolves, however, designers provide developers with input on the implementation of certain features, ensuring the proper evolution of their vision. These conversations promote transparency of process and progress. This transparency builds bonds between team members. Teammates who trust each other are more motivated to work together to produce higher-quality work.

Collaborative Design in Practice

In 2010, I was designing a dashboard for a web app targeted at TheLadders' recruiter and employer audience. There was a lot of information to fit on one screen and I was struggling to make it all work. Instead of burning too much time at my desk pushing pixels, I grabbed a whiteboard and called the lead developer over. I sketched my original idea about how to lay out all the content and functionality for this dashboard. We discussed it and then I handed him the marker. He sketched his ideas on the same whiteboard. We went back and forth, ultimately converging on a layout and interaction schema that was not only usable but feasible given our two-week sprint timeframes (see Figure 4-2). At the end of that two-hour session, we returned to our desks and started working. I refined our sketch into a more formal wireframe and workflow and he began to write the infrastructure code necessary to get the data we needed to the presentation layer.

We had built a shared understanding through our collaborative design session. We both knew what we were going to build and what it needed to do. We didn't need to wait to document it. This approach allowed us to get the first version of this idea built within our two-week timeframe.

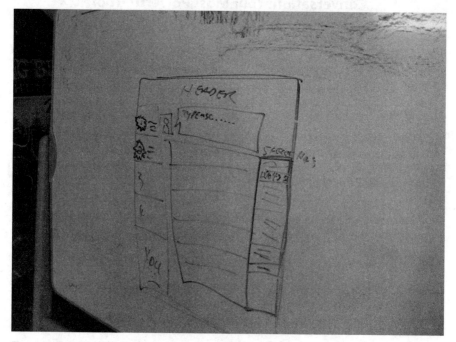

Figure 4-2. *Whiteboard sketch that we arrived at together.*

CHAPTER 4

Design Studio

When your team is comfortable collaborating, informal sessions like the one I've just described take place all the time. But sometimes you are going to need to gather everyone for a formal working session. Design Studio is a popular way to do this. Design Studio (sometimes called Design Charrette) is a way to bring a cross-functional team together to visualize potential solutions to a design problem. It breaks down organizational silos and creates a forum for your fellow teammates' points of view. By putting designers, developers, subject matter experts, product managers, business analysts, and other competencies together in the same space, and focusing them all on the same challenge, you create an outcome far greater than working in silos allows. A Design Studio has another benefit: it starts to build the trust your team will need to move from these formal sessions to more frequent and informal collaborations.

Running a Design Studio

Although the technique described below is very specific, you should feel comfortable to run less or more formal Design Studios as your situation and timing warrants. The specifics of the ritual are not the end goal: instead, you should be aiming to solve problems with your colleagues and clients.

Process

Design Studio follows this path:

1. Problem definition and constraints

2. Individual idea generation (diverge)

3. Presentation and critique

4. Iterate and refine (emerge)

5. Team idea generation (converge)

Supplies

Here's what you'll need:

- Pencils

- Pens

- Permanent markers (multiple colors/thicknesses)

- Highlighters (multiple colors)

- Sketching templates (you can use preprinted 1-up and 6-up templates or you can use blank sheets of 11"×17" paper divided into six boxes)

- 25"×30.5" self-stick easel pads

- Drafting dots (or any kind of small stickers)

The process works best for a team of five to eight people. If you have more people, create more teams and have the teams compare output at the end of the process.

Problem definition and constraints (15–45 minutes)

The first step in Design Studio is to ensure that everyone is aware of the problem you are trying to solve, the assumptions you've declared (including personas, as explained elsewhere in this chapter), the hypotheses you've generated, and the constraints within which you are working. This step can be anything from a formal presentation with slides to a group discussion, based on the team's level of comfort.

Individual idea generation (10 minutes)

You'll be working individually in this step. Give each member of the team a 6-up template—a sheet of paper with six empty boxes on it (Figure 4-3). You can make one by folding a blank sheet of 11"×17" paper (or you can use a preprinted template).

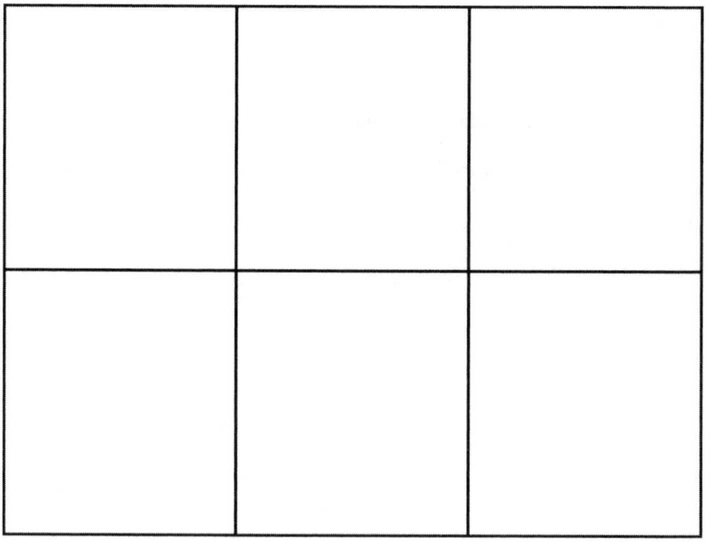

Figure 4-3. *A 6-up template.*

Optional: sometimes, people find they have hard time facing a blank page. If that's the case, try the following step (5 minutes): ask each person to label each box of his or her sheet with one of your personas and the specific pain point or problem he will be addressing for that persona. Write the persona's name and pain point at the top of each of the six boxes. Team members can write the same persona/pain point pair as many times as they have solutions for that problem, or they can write a different persona/pain point combination for each box. Any combination works.

Next, with your blank (or optionally labeled) 6-up sheets in front of you, give everyone five minutes to generate six low-fidelity sketches of solutions for each persona/pain point pair on their 6-up. These should be visual articulations (UI sketches, workflows, diagrams, etc.), not written words. Encourage your team by revealing the dirty secret of interaction design to level the playing field: if you can draw a circle, a square, and a triangle, you can draw every interface. I'm confident that everyone on your team can draw those shapes.

Presentation and critique (3 minutes per person)

When time is up, share and critique what you've done so far (see Figure 4-4). Going around the table, give each participant three minutes to hold up his or her sketches and present them to the team. Presenters should explicitly state for whom they were solving a problem (persona), which pain point they were addressing (hypothesis), then explain the sketch. Each member of the team should provide critique and feedback to the presenter. Critique should focus on clarifying the presenter's intentions. Questions such as "How does this feature address the persona's specific problem?" are very helpful. Comments such as "I don't like that idea" provide little value and don't give the presenter concrete ideas for iterating.

Make sure that every team member presents and receives critique.

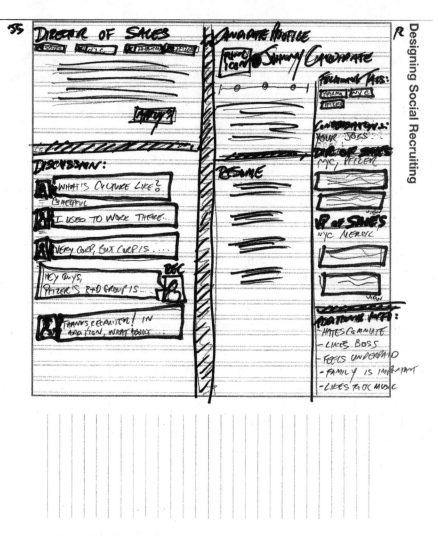

Figure 4-4. *Example of typical Design Studio output.*

Iterate and refine (5–10 minutes)

Now ask everyone to work individually once more. Ask each participant to take his or her original six ideas and, using the critique they just received, to refine their thinking into one big idea on a single sheet of 11"×17" paper. The goal here is to pick the idea that has the most merit and develop a more evolved version of that idea.

Once time is up, ask the team to go through the present and critique process again.

Team idea generation (45 minutes)

Now that everyone on the team has feedback on his or her individual idea, the team must converge on one idea. In this step, the team is trying to converge on the idea they feel has the biggest chance for success. This idea will serve as the basis for the next step in the Lean UX process: creating an MVP and running experiments (both covered in the next chapter).

Ask the team to use a large 2'×3' self-stick easel pad or a whiteboard to sketch the components and workflow for their idea. There will be a lot of compromise and wrangling at this stage; to get to consensus, the team will need to prioritize and pare back features. Encourage the team to create a "parking lot" for good ideas that don't make the cut, which will make it easier to let go of ideas.

If you have multiple teams in the design studio, ask each team to present their final idea to the room when they are finished for one final round of critique and feedback.

The artifacts created in the design studio are now used to create refined wireframes, prototypes, and early code that will drive the team forward in proving their hypotheses.

Style Guides

One tool that makes collaborative design easier is the style guide. A style guide is a broadly accepted pattern library that codifies the interactive, visual, and copy elements of a user interface and system. Style guides (also known as pattern libraries) are a living collection of all of your product's customer-facing components. If it's made of pixels, it goes in the style guide. Headers, footers, grids, forms, labels, button logic, and everything else that goes into your product's user experience goes in the style guide.

Some companies use wikis for their style guides, which allows the collection to stay current and accessible to everyone on the team. Other teams choose to create "live" style guides. These are repositories of front-end code and design that not only define how the product looks and behaves, but actually function as the underlying markup and stylesheets for that experience. If you change the style guide, you change the product.

Style guides create efficiency. They provide a repository of ready-to-go, approved interface components that can be assembled and aligned to form a workflow. By minimizing debate over mundane elements like the placement of labels in forms or the never-ending debate over left/right placement of the "positive" action button, developers can get started creating core UI components without waiting for a designer to define and specify these assets. The assets are already designed, defined, and collected in one place.

Interaction and visual designers benefit as well. They no longer have to recreate representations of experiences that already exist. They become free to focus on new design challenges—novel interaction problems or extending the visual system to new elements. Approval cycles are streamlined because the repetitive elements (e.g., the treatment of the global navigation) are no longer up for debate. Reviews become more focused on the core product challenge and broader views of the proposed solution.

Creating a Style Guide

There are two basic approaches to creating a style guide:

Big bang

> In this approach, your team takes a limited amount of time (e.g., one to two weeks or sometimes months) away from their current efforts to document all of your product's UI elements in a style guide. The benefit here is that the style guide gets created in a relatively short amount of time. The negative is that your team is not learning anything new about your product during this time.

Slow drip

> In this approach, your team adds an element to the style guide each time they create or change one for the project. The biggest benefit here is that the team continues to work on the project. However, the drawback is that the style guide is rarely completed and therefore fails to provide some of the efficiencies that a complete one does.

Maintaining a Style Guide

When planning your style guide, it's important to plan for maintenance. You're going to need to create a process and dedicate people to keeping your style guide up to date. Think of a style guide as a living process that you launch and maintain, rather than a static thing you create. When you have an up-to-date and easy-to-use style guide, you make it easy for the team to actually use the style guide—and your goal should be to make it easier to use the style guide than to avoid it. You want to make compliance easy! So plan to dedicate people and time to keeping your style guide current.

Case Study

In this case study, we'll look at how the UX team at General Electric (GE) created an enterprise-grade style guide.

When Greg Petroff took the helm of GE's global UX practice in late 2011, he inherited a globally distributed team struggling to bring great product experiences to one of the world's largest organizations. As it turns out, GE is the fourteenth-largest producer of software in the world, creating systems to monitor, manage, and understand the industrial equipment they build. With 500 developers for every designer, the team found it challenging to achieve the desired design results to satisfy the organization's massive demands. Hiring more designers was not an option, and broad corporate advocacy for increased consideration of UX design methods would change cultural foundations—including processes, values, communications practices, attitudes, and assumptions—too slowly. In addition, the newly minted UX Center of Excellence quickly found itself overwhelmed by requests for work. Reviewing every UX project that came through the company had turned them into the bottleneck they were seeking to remove.

There had to be a better way. The team initially tried to build a company-wide UX community through a centralized social networking platform. Although that approach began to build camaraderie, it didn't do enough to socialize a consistent design aesthetic or enable development teams without UX capability to do good work.

After running a few pilot projects across several business lines, Petroff's team quickly noticed recurring use cases, personas, and design patterns. With individual business lines focused on their business needs and not on the whole, there was naturally a tremendous amount of duplicative work being done at GE, as each separate organization recreated similar elements over and over. Worse, the quality of that work had not progressed to what smartphone customers were starting to demand. GE's method was not only inefficient, it was also increasing the amount of time each project took to reach market. And when projects did reach market, the experiences across GE business lines were disparate and inconsistent.

The team brainstormed over the course of a week and came up with a straw man of what a social environment for consistent UX guidelines would look like. Their target audience was GE's 8,000 software engineers worldwide. The team realized that by empowering the developers with templates, guidelines, assets, and code snippets, they could take great UX into their own hands without waiting for design assistance or approval.

With that initiative, the Industrial Internet Design System (IIDS) was born. The straw man was greenlighted by management and was implemented over the summer of 2012.

The IIDS is based on modern HTML5 frameworks such as Bootstrap, jQuery, and others, but looks nothing like them (see Figures 4-5 and 4-6). It is a branded, functional UI design pattern library. It provides the graphical assets, code snippets, and usage rules for each of GE's templated product experiences. The team also built example applications to aid other teams in the composition of applications. The IIDS also includes typical customer personas so that project teams can get a clear sense of their target customers and how the intended customer affects the design pattern choices they make.

Petroff's team identified two distinct audiences for the IIDS. The first was developers at GE who need the assets to build sites and products. The second was made up of the program managers and owners who need to decide what kind of application to create. The IIDS serves both communities well, with positive feedback coming in regularly, usage statistics skyrocketing, and project-success metrics going up and to the right.

The IIDS is empowering teams seeking to become more agile and dip their toes into Lean Startup. It allows project teams to build prototypes of experiences far faster than ever before. These prototypes reach the validation stages months earlier than projects in the past, allowing the teams to prove their worth well in advance of heavy back-end integration. Average project lifecycles have been shortened by as much as six months with rough estimated resource-usage savings in the millions per year.

Most importantly, all the teams at GE are now empowered to get to a clickable version of their experience in days instead of months. They are able to bring these ideas to internal stakeholders and external customers well before committing further resources. In addition, the teams are far better equipped to judge how successful a new product release will be. The waste that once plagued the product design cycle in GE is slowly being alleviated through the ever-improving resources available in the IIDS.

Figure 4-5. *An example of the IIDS template page.*

My Application

Dashboard   Fleet

Asset 001 Name/ID

Overview | Events | **Data**

Filter ▾ | ★ Filter One ✕

>	Site Name	Site Name	Site Name	Site Name	Site Name ↓	Numerical Data	Site Name	Site Name	Site Name
>	Lost Coast	Great Land	Great Land	Great Land	Great Land	10.05	Great Land	Great Land	Great Land
>	Great Land	Lost Coast	Great Land	Great Land	Great Land	215.05	Great Land	Great Land	Great Land
>	Great Land	Great Land	Lost Coast	Great Land	Great Land	1589.09	Great Land	Great Land	Great Land
>	Great Land	Great Land	Great Land	Lost Coast	Great Land	10.05	Cliff Island	Great Land	Great Land
>	Great Land	Great Land	Great Land	Great Land	Lost Coast	215.05	Peaks Island	Great Land	Great Land
>	Great Land	Great Land	Great Land	Great Land	Great Land	1589.09	Lost Coast	Great Land	Great Land
>	Great Land	Great Land	Great Land	Great Land	Great Land	10.05	Great Land	Lost Coast	Great Land
>	Great Land	Great Land	Great Land	Great Land	Great Land	215.05	Great Land	Great Land	Lost Coast
>	Great Land	Great Land	Diamond	Great Land	Great Land	1589.09	Great Land	Great Land	Great Land
>	Great Land	Great Land	Great Land	Great Land	Great Land	10.05	Great Land	Great Land	Great Land
>	Great Land	Great Land	Great Land	Great Land	Great Land	215.05	Great Land	Great Land	Great Land
>	Great Land	Great Land	Great Land	Great Land	Great Land	1589.09	Great Land	Great Land	Great Land
>	Great Land	Great Land	Great Land	Great Land	Great Land	10.05	Great Land	Great Land	Great Land
>	Great Land	Great Land	Great Land	Great Land	Great Land	215.05	Great Land	Great Land	Great Land
>	Great Land	Great Land	Great Land	Great Land	Great Land	1589.09	Great Land	Great Land	Great Land
>	Great Land	Great Land	Great Land	Great Land	Great Land	10.05	Great Land	Great Land	Great Land

Show 50 ▾ entries

1 – 50 of 495 ← 1 2 3 4 5 →

Figure 4-6. *A table layout in the IIDS.*

What Goes Into a Style Guide?

If it's made of pixels, it goes into the style guide. All *interaction design* elements should be defined and added to the style guide. Use design patterns that work well in your existing product as the baseline of your style guide. Form fields, labels, drop-down menus, radio button placement and behavior, Ajax and jQuery events, buttons—all should be included in the style guide.

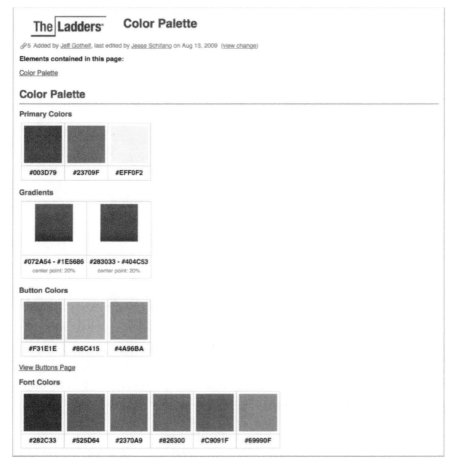

Figure 4-7. *Style guide example from TheLadders.*

Provide three data points for each interaction design element:

What the element looks like

> Include detail about the minimum and maximum sizes of the element, vertical and horizontal constraints, and any styling demands on the element.

Where it's usually placed on the screen

> Make it clear if an element should be consistently placed in certain areas of the screen as well as any exceptions that may negate this design pattern.

When it should be used

> It's imperative that your team knows when to use a drop-down menu rather than a radio button and other factors that would determine the selection of one UI element over another.

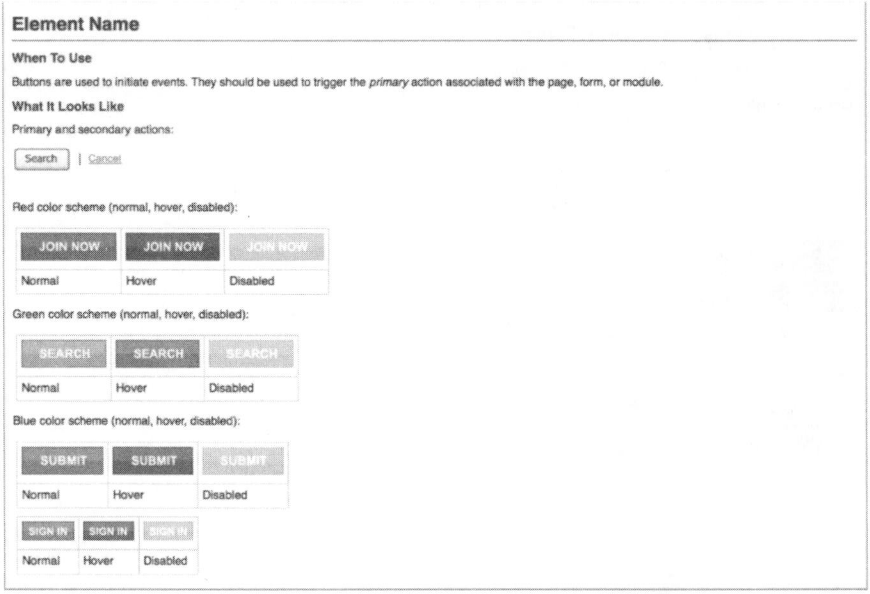

Figure 4-8. *Another example of a style guide page from TheLadders.*

Next, include all *visual design* elements. Start with the general color palette of your product. Ensure that each primary color is available with hex values as well as complementary and secondary color choices. If certain elements, such as buttons, have different colors based on state, ensure that this information is included. Other elements to include here are logos, headers, footers, grid structures, and typographical choices (i.e., which fonts to use where and at what size/weight). The same attributes of what, where, and when provided for interaction design elements should also be included here.

Finally, ensure that *copywriting* styles are codified as well. Capture the tone of your brand, specific words you will and won't use, grammatical choices, tolerated (and not tolerated) colloquialisms, along with button language (OK? Yes? Go? etc.) and other navigation language (previous/next, more/less, etc.).

Characteristics of a Successful Style Guide

A successful style guide has three important characteristics: it's *accessible*, it's *continually improved* (a.k.a. a living document), and it's *actionable*.

Accessible

Accessibility means that the style guide is available to everyone in your organization. Accessible style guides are:

Easily found

Use a memorable URL and ensure that everyone is aware of it.

Easily distributed

Ensure that your teams can access the style guides at their convenience (in the office, out of the office, on mobile, etc.).

Easy to search

A comprehensive and accurate search feature in the style guide greatly increases its usage.

Easy to use

Treat this as you would any other design project. If it's not usable, it will go unused very quickly.

Continually improved

The style guide should be considered a living document. Yes, the elements within it ensure a consistent experience for your customers, but your product (and your customers) will evolve. The style guide should be malleable enough to add these updates easily. In addition, as your designers create new elements, they will demand an easy way to add them to the style guide.

I recommend using a wiki. Here's why:

- Wikis are familiar places for developers. This means that getting your teammates in engineering to participate in this tool will not involve forcing them to learn a new tool or one that was purpose-built only for designers.

- Wikis keep revision histories (good ones do, anyway). This practice is crucial because there will be times when you want to roll back updates to the UI. Revision histories keep you from having to recreate previous states of the style guide.

- Wikis keep track of who changed what and provide commenting functionality. This feature is ideal for keeping a trail of what decisions were made, who made them, and the rationale for and even the discussion about making that change. As you bring on board new team members, this type of historical capture can bring them up to speed much faster. In other words, wikis are your documentation.

Actionable

Your style guide is not just a library or museum for interaction components. It should be a "widget factory" that can produce any interface element on demand. As each new element is added to the style guide, make it available for download in whatever formats your team will need. Ensure that not only the code is available but the graphical and wireframe assets as well. Doing so allows every designer to have a full palette of interface elements with which to create prototypes at any given time.

How Do You Create a Style Guide?

There are two parts to creating a style guide:

1. *Create a table of contents (TOC)*—the TOC determines how your style guide will be structured and provides buckets into which you can start dropping design elements. Separate your TOC into interaction design, visual design, copywriting, branding guidelines, accessibility needs, and any other high-level sections that make sense for your business.

2. *Populate the content*—As mentioned earlier, there are two ways to go about this: the big bang approach and the slow drip.

   The *big bang* approach (in which your team creates the entire style guide in advance of any project) works well if you have a young product or a relatively simple one.

   The *slow drip* approach works well if you have a legacy or complex product.

Maintaining a Style Guide

Your style guide must stay current if it's to stay relevant and useful. Add new experiences as they're created and remove outdated features as they are deprecated.

Assign an owner to the style guide. That person need not be singlehandedly responsible for the creation of content in the style guide itself, but he or she should be responsible for ensuring the current state of the guide. Your style guide curator should reach out to content creators and ensure that elements are entered as they are created. In essence, this person functions as the editor of the pattern library. It's a less than enviable position, so consider rotating this role on a regular basis every three months.

Not Just for Designers

Your style guide should not contain information relevant only to designers. It must house code snippets as well. Developers then have a one-stop shop for getting all their design direction as well as foundational pieces of code that will get them to some kind of experience exponentially faster than before.

A Word about Live Style Guides

Teams working on the Web have recently begun taking a new approach to style guides—the live style guide. Essentially, these are identical to wiki-based style guides, with one fundamental difference: the code in a live style guide is the same code the application uses. Teams gain efficiencies from this approach but take on some additional infrastructure and process burden.

Live style guides are basically a portion of your product that is visible only to the product team. It is a portion of your application that generates a "one of each" page that displays all the styles and widgets being used on the site. It has the advantage of being much closer to self-maintaining.

As you make changes to the underlying HTML and CSS of your site, these changes are displayed in the style guide pages. Someone still needs to pay attention to this page to make sure it's curated and maintained and that conflicts are resolved. But the movement toward a self-documented application is exciting and holds tremendous promise.

Collaborating with Geographically Distributed Teams

Physical distance is one of the biggest challenges to strong collaboration. Some of the methods I've discussed in this chapter—especially Design Studio—become harder when a team isn't all in the same location. But you can still find ways to collaborate.

Here are some techniques that can help bridge the distance for geographically distributed teams. Tools such as Skype, Google Docs (including Google Draw), wikis, and a phone with a camera make cross-time-zone collaboration effective and allow teams to feel virtually connected for long periods of time during the day.

Worldwide Collaborative Design Session

Geographically distributed teams make collaborative design more difficult. But the benefits are worth the extra effort. Let's take a look at how one team with whom I worked overcame a continent-wide separation and designed solutions together.

This team was divided into two groups in two cities: the product and user experience team was in New York and the development team was in Vancouver. My goal was to run a Design Studio and affinity mapping session with the whole team.

Setup

We asked the two groups to gather in their individual conference rooms with their own laptops. Each conference room had a Mac in it with a location-specific Skype account (i.e., it wasn't a specific individual's account, it was that office's account). The two offices connected to each other via their office Skype accounts so that we could see each other as a group. This step was critical, as it was the closest we could get to physically being in the same room.

We prepared a very brief setup presentation (about 10 slides) that explained the problem statement we were tackling. It included customer testimonials, data, and a very brief recap of our customers' needs. The presentation also included the constraints of the solution space.

Priming the pump with affinity mapping

We kicked things off with an affinity mapping exercise. Typically these are done with sticky notes and a whiteboard. In this case, we used a shared Google Docs spreadsheet to conduct the exercise. We asked everyone in both offices to sign in to the shared spreadsheet. The spreadsheet itself had a column labeled for each person. Google Docs allows multiple editors to work in the same document. In this case, we had eight team members in the document at the same time!

We asked the team to come up with as many ideas as they could think of to solve the problem we presented. Each team member wrote one idea per cell in the column marked with his or her name. We gave them five minutes to generate as many ideas as they could.

In order to make sure that everyone in each location was aware of all of the proposals, we next asked each team member to read his or her ideas to the distributed team. Some ideas went by quickly and others generated more discussion.

To simulate affinity grouping in the shared spreadsheet, the facilitator (me, in this case) began a second sheet in the document using a personal laptop. I created some initial column headers in the second sheet that reflected themes I was hearing as the group read their ideas.

Then I asked the team to take each idea and copy it into the matching theme on the second sheet. If it didn't fit, I asked them to create their own theme. I also encouraged them to change the wording of the themes as we went along if they felt the theme name was either not representative or misleading.

At the end of this process, we had a spreadsheet filled with ideas that were sorted into themes. Some themes had just a pair of ideas; others had as many as eight.

App Quality - "Dump and Sort" ☆

File   Edit   View   Insert   Format   Data   Tools   Help   Last edit was made 2 days ago by jun

	A	B	C	
1	Loc	Maia	Neng	Joseph
2				Create a use application f(user's point (see the curre form and ma mandatory. I is provided (they can cho that they car way it looks
3	Make sure that NT know what the requirements are	sort things into categories!!! so that we don't overwhelm them with choices. Have a refinement option for braod choices, eg if a country is selected, then the option to select regions will show. http://www.ted.com/talks/she	collect opinions from groups as many as possible, so we know more factors from target users' point of views.	would be pre entrepreneur
	allow investors to preview applications from NT perspective	make the effect of selections changes obvious to users, eg have an possiblity to render an example of the customized application form	let the entrepreneurs aware that his application will be filtered by gust, according to criteria set up by the relevant groups. So he will be cautious to provide more relevant data.	Allow anyon(see the appl correspondir group.
4			this filter functionality needs to be re-usable for searching for potential enternrises	Post the app sample, with on the group entrepreneur they're up a(printable PD

Figure 4-9. *Output of a remote affinity mapping session.*

Design Studio with remote teams

To set up for the next step, a Design Studio session, we tried to mimic a co-located version of the activity as much as possible. We distributed paper and pens to each location. We created a dual-monitor setup in each conference room so that each room would be able to see the sketches on one monitor while still being able to see their teammates via Skype on the second monitor (as shown in Figure 4-10). We asked each team to use an iPhone to photograph their sketches and email them to everyone else. This setup helped connect the dialog and the artifacts to the conversation.

After that initial setup, we were able to proceed with the Design Studio process as usual. Each team member was able to present his or her ideas to both rooms and to receive transcontinental critique. The two teams were able to refine their ideas together and were eventually able to converge on one idea to take forward.

Figure 4-10. *Dual monitor setup during remote Design Studio.*

Wrapping Up: Collaborative Design

Collaborative design is the evolution of UX. In this chapter, I discussed how "open sourcing" the design process brings the entire team deeper into the project. I talked about how the low-fidelity drawings created in Design Studio sessions can help teams generate many ideas and then converge on a set the entire team can get behind. I showed you practical techniques that you can use to create shared understanding, the fundamental currency of Lean UX. Using tools such as style guides, Design Studio, and simple conversation, your team members can build a shared understanding that allows them to move forward at a much faster pace than in traditional environments.

Now that all of our assumptions are declared and our design hypotheses created, you can really get into the learning process. In the next chapter, I cover the Minimum Viable Product (MVP) and how to use it to plan experiments. We'll use those experiments to test the validity of our assumptions and decide how to move forward with our project.

CHAPTER 5

MVPs and Experiments

*All life is an experiment. The more
experiments you make, the better.*

Ralph Waldo Emerson

With the parts of your hypothesis now defined, you're ready to determine which product ideas are valid and which ones you should discard. In this chapter, we discuss the Minimum Viable Product (MVP) and what it means in Lean UX. In addition, we'll cover:

- Determining product focus (delivering value or increasing learning?) using MVP

- Using prototypes and prototyping tools

- Running experiments without prototypes

About MVPs and Experiments

Lean UX makes heavy use of the notion of MVP. MVPs help test our assumptions—will this tactic achieve the desired outcome?—while minimizing the work we put into unproven ideas. The sooner we can find which features are worth investing in, the sooner we can focus our limited resources on the best solutions to our business problems. This concept is an important part of how Lean UX minimizes waste.

Your prioritized list of hypotheses has given you several paths to explore. To do this exploration, you are going to want to create the smallest thing you can to determine the validity of each of these hypothesis statements. That is your MVP. You will use your MVP to run experiments. The outcome of the experiments will tell you whether your hypothesis was correct and thus whether the direction you are exploring should be pursued, refined, or abandoned.

The Focus of an MVP

The phrase MVP has caused a lot of confusion in its short life. The problem is that it gets used in two different ways. Sometimes teams create an MVP primarily to learn something. They're not concerned with delivering value to the market; they're just trying to figure out what the market wants. In other cases, teams create a small version of a product or a feature because they want to start delivering value to the market as quickly as possible. In this second case, if you design and deploy the MVP correctly, you should also be able to learn from it, even if that's not the primary focus. See Figure 5-1.

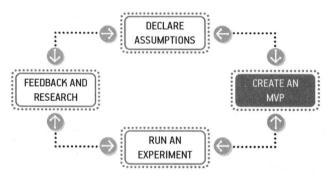

Figure 5-1. *You will create MVPs after you've defined and prioritized a set of hypotheses.*

Let's take as an example a medium-sized company with which I consulted recently. They were exploring new marketing tactics and wanted to launch a monthly newsletter. Newsletter creation is no small task. You need to prepare a content strategy, editorial calendar, layout and design, as well as an ongoing marketing strategy. You need writers and editors to work on it. All in all, it's a big expenditure for the company to undertake. The team decided to treat this newsletter idea as a hypothesis.

The first question they had to answer was whether there enough customer demand for a newsletter to justify the effort. The MVP they used to test the idea was a signup form on their current website. The signup form promoted the newsletter and asked for a customer's email address. This approach wouldn't deliver any value to the customer—yet. Instead, the focus was on helping the team learn enough to make a good decision about whether to proceed.

They spent half a day designing and coding the form and were able to launch it that same afternoon. The team knew that their site received a significant amount of traffic each day: they would be able to learn very quickly if there was interest in their newsletter.

At this point, the team made no effort to design or build the actual newsletter. That would come later, after the team had gathered enough data to make a GO/NO-GO decision. After the team had gathered enough data, and if the data showed that their customers wanted the newsletter, the team would move on to their next MVP, one that would begin to deliver value and learning. They planned to experiment with MVP versions of the newsletter itself that would let them test content strategy, design, and other newsletter features.

Creating an MVP

When you start planning your MVP, the first thing you have to do is consider what you're trying to learn. It's useful to think about these three basic questions:

1. Is there a need for the solution I'm designing?

2. Is there value in the solution and features I'm offering?

3. Is my solution usable?

Although you can build an MVP to help you answer any of these questions, the first question is probably best answered with traditional design research methods. (In the next chapter, we discuss Lean approaches to this research.) But for the second and third questions, using an MVP adds a lot of value.

If you're trying to answer question two, you will likely find yourself creating an MVP that is optimized for learning. If your question is about the usability of your solution, you will want to emphasize value delivery in your product. This step will allow you to "release" a product into the market and "observe" users interacting with it in realistic contexts.

Here are some guidelines to follow if you're trying to maximize your learning:

Be clear and concise

> Spend your time distilling your idea to its core value proposition and present that to your customers

Prioritize ruthlessly

Ideas, like artifacts, are transient. Let the best ones prove themselves.

Stay agile

Information will come in quickly, so make sure that you're working in a medium that allows you to make updates easily.

Measure behavior

Build MVPs that allow you to observe and measure what people actually *do*, not just what people say. In digital product design, behavior trumps opinion.

Use a call-to-action

You will know people value your solution when they demonstrate that they are using it. A call-to-action is a clear phrase, sometimes complemented by an image, that asks the user to take a specific action: "sign up" or "buy now." Giving people a way to opt in to or sign up for a service is a great way to know if they're interested.

Here are some guidelines to follow if you're trying to deliver value to your customers:

Be functional

Some level of integration with the rest of your application must be in place to create a realistic usage scenario.

Integrate with existing analytics

Measuring the performance of your MVP must be done within the context of existing product workflows.

Be consistent with the rest of the application

To minimize any biases toward the new functionality, design your MVP to fit with your current style guide and brand.

Of course, you'll find that you're trying to learn and deliver value at the same time. Keeping these guidelines in mind as you plan your MVPs will help you navigate the trade-offs and compromises you're going to have to make.

Regardless of your desired outcome, build the smallest MVP possible. Remember that it is a tool for learning. You will be iterating. You will be modifying it. You may very well be throwing it away entirely.

And keep one last thing in mind: in many cases, your MVP won't involve any code at all. Instead, you will rely on many of the UX designer's existing tools: sketching, prototyping, copywriting, and visual design.

Prototyping

One of the most effective ways to create MVP's is by prototyping the experience. A prototype is an approximation of an experience that allows you to simulate what it is like to use the product or service in question. It needs to be clickable (or tappable). At the same time, your goal should be to expend as little effort as possible in order to create the prototype, which makes your choice of prototyping tool important.

Choosing which tool to use for your prototype depends on:

- Who will be interacting with it
- What you hope to learn
- How much time you have to create it

It's critical to specify the intended audience for your prototype. Knowing your audience allows you to create the smallest possible prototype that will generate meaningful feedback from this audience. For example, if you're using the prototype primarily to demo ideas to software engineers on your team, the prototype can largely overlook primary areas of the product that aren't being affected by the prototype, such as the global navigation. Your developers know those items are there and that they're not changing, so you don't need to illustrate those items for them.

Stakeholders, often less familiar with their own product than they'll ever admit, will likely need a greater level of fidelity in the prototype in order to truly grasp the concept. To meet the various needs of these disparate audiences, your prototyping toolkit should be fairly broad. You'll want a broad range of methods to communicate your ideas. Let's take a look at some ways to create prototypes and the pros and cons of each.

Low-Fidelity Prototypes: Paper

Made of the most accessible components—paper, pens, and tape—paper prototypes (Figure 5-2) allow you to simulate experiences in a quick, crafty, fun manner. No digital investment is necessary. Using tactics such as flaps to show and hide different states on a page or even creating a "window" for a slideshow of images to move through gives the team a sense of how the product should function. You'll be able to get an immediate sense of what is available in the experience and what is missing. Paper prototyping can give you a sense of how the workflow is starting to coalesce around the interface elements you've assembled. Paper prototyping is especially helpful with touch interfaces that require the user to manipulate elements on a screen.

Figure 5-2. *Example of paper prototype.*

Pros

- Can be created in an hour
- Easily arranged and rearranged
- Cheap
- Can be assembled with materials already found in the office
- Fun activity that many people enjoy

Cons

- Rapid iteration and duplication of the prototype can become time-consuming and tedious
- The simulation is very artificial, because you're not using the actual input mechanisms (mouse, trackpad, keyboard, touch screen, etc.)
- Feedback is limited to the high-level structure and flow of the product

Low-Fidelity Prototypes: Clickable Wireframes

Creating an experience with clickable wireframes (Figure 5-3) lets you take a prototype to the next level of fidelity. Your investment in pixels provides a bit more realistic feel to the workflow. Test participants and team members use digital input mechanisms to interact with the prototype, which offers better insight and feedback about the way they will interact with the product at the level of the click, tap, or gesture.

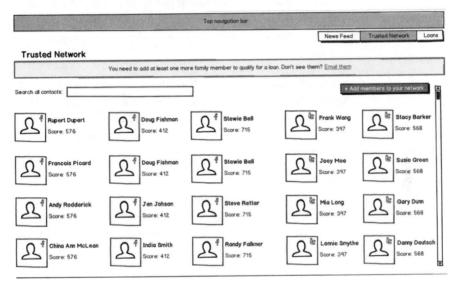

Figure 5-3. *Clickable wireframe prototype example.*

Pros

- Provides a good sense of the length of workflow

- Reveals major obstacles to primary task completion

- Allows assessment of findability of core elements

- Can be used to quickly create "something clickable" to get your team learning from your existing assets instead of forcing the creation of new ones

Cons

- Most people who will interact with these assets are savvy enough to recognize an unfinished product

- More attention than normal is paid to labeling and copy

Tools for creating low-fidelity clickable wireframes

Here are some of the tools that work well for this type of prototyping:

Balsamiq

> An inexpensive wireframing tool that provides "sketchy"-looking output. It's the closest thing to digital sketching of interfaces and has a robust community of support. Its limitations are what make it powerful; you can't spend your time tweaking the finer points of the interface, so you spend more time churning through revisions. The ability to link pages together easily makes it a great early prototyping tool.

Microsoft Visio

> This program, the granddaddy of wireframing tools, can still be used to link its screens together to create something clickable. It's hard to work quickly with Visio, though: the general challenges of using this product make it less and less attractive as more modern products, both desktop and web-based, enter the market.

OmniGraffle (Mac only)

> In many ways, this is the Mac equivalent of Visio, though it is easier to use, has more robust features, and provides better-looking artifacts. You can use images in your drawings, so you can create good-looking artifacts. Still, its core power is in diagramming, not in simulating workflows and interaction.

Microsoft PowerPoint

> In a pinch, PowerPoint can still be relied on to fake some level of interactivity. You can use the native drawing tools to draw wireframes and link them together, or you can import mockups, wireframes, or screenshots that you've created in another tool. By clicking sequentially through your slides or by using linked hotspots, you can provide a bare minimum level of fake interactivity. On the Mac, Keynote can be used in the same way. You can also buy libraries of images from Keynotopia that let you assemble realistic-looking mockups. Maintaining these prototypes can end up being very time-consuming.

Fluid Designer/Pop Prototype on Paper

> These mobile prototytping tools (and others like them, which are emerging very rapidly) allow you to quickly build prototypes that run on a smartphone. You import images (or photograph sketches) and link them quickly using hotspots. You can simulate simple workflows very quickly.

Mid- and High Fidelity Prototypes

Mid- and high-fidelity prototypes (see Figure 5-4) have significantly more detail than wireframe-based prototypes. You'll use these to demonstrate and test designs that are fleshed out with a level of interaction, visual, and /or content design that is similar to (or indistinguishable from) the final product experience. The level of interactivity that you can create at this level varies from tool to tool; however, most tools in this category allow you to represent pixel-perfect simulations of the final experience. You will be able to create interface elements such as forms, fields, drop-down menus that work, and form buttons that simulate submit actions. Some tools allow logical branching and basic data operations. Many allow some types of minor animations, transitions, and state changes. Additionally, the cost of creating this level of fidelity is significantly reduced with the use of these tools.

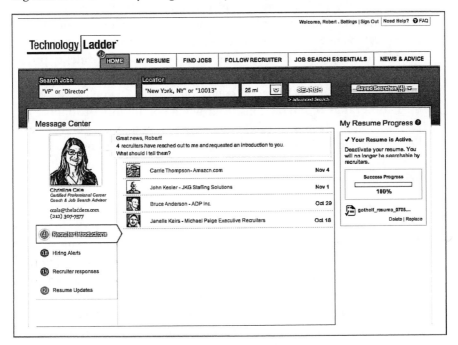

Figure 5-4. *Example of a mid-fidelity prototype.*

Pros

- Produces high-quality and realistic prototypes
- Visual design and brand elements can be tested
- Workflow and user interface interactions can be assessed

Cons

- Interactivity is still more limited than fully native prototypes
- Users typically can't interact with real data, so there is a limit to the types of product interactions you can simulate
- Depending on the tool, it can be time-consuming to create and maintain these prototypes; maintaining a high-fidelity prototype and keeping it in sync with the actual product often involves duplicate effort

Tools for creating mid- and high-fidelity clickable wireframes

Here are some of the tools that work well for this type of prototyping (again, this is only a very partial list):

Axure RP

This increasingly popular prototyping tool allows you to create realistic web pages with screens and forms, and to submit workflows. Axure mockups run in any browser and do an excellent job of simulating web pages. Because it imports images well and supports native HTML user interface elements, it is a very effective mid-fidelity prototyping tool (though you can use it for both low- and high-fidelity prototypes as well). It has good conditional logic, so you can mock up a good range of interactions. A growing community of support is sprouting up around Axure, and many interaction designers have begun using it as their primary tool. Its ability to generate specifications from the prototype is an added bonus for organizations that still make those demands of their teams.

Adobe Fireworks

An old Macromedia acquisition, Fireworks tries to blend the best of Adobe Illustrator with the best of Photoshop and mashes it up in a stew of pseudo-interactivity that makes it a powerful prototyping tool when visual fidelity is important. You can create screens and manage varying states of specific elements. You can add working form components. You can link elements via simple hotspots. You can create custom asset libraries that make the reuse of interface elements efficient and encourage use of the tool.

Coded Prototypes

Coded prototypes offer the highest level of fidelity for simulated experiences. For all intents and purposes, people interacting with this type of prototype should not be able to distinguish it from the final product unless they bump up against the limits of its scope (i.e., they click on a link to a page that was not prototyped). Coded prototypes exist in the native environment (the browser, the OS, on the device, etc.) and make use of all of the expected interactive elements. Buttons, drop-down menus, and form fields all function as the user would expect them to. These prototypes take input from the mouse, keyboard, and screen. They create as natural an interaction pattern as possible for the prototype's evaluators.

Hand-coded and live-data prototypes

There are two levels of fidelity for coded prototypes: hand-coded and live data. The hand-coded prototypes look and function like the end product, but don't account for any kind of real-time data input, processing, or output. They are still just simulations. The live-data prototypes will connect with real-time data and process user input. These are often deployed to real customers and offer a level of analytical insight into customers' usage of the prototype that is not available from hand-coded prototypes. They can also be used when A/B testing certain features or changes to the current workflow.

Pros

- Potential to reuse code for production

- The most realistic simulation to create

- Can be generated from existing code assets

Cons

- Team can get bogged down in debating the finer points of the prototype

- Time-consuming to create working code that delivers the desired experience

- Tempting to perfect the code before releasing to customers

- Updating and iterating can take a lot of time

What Should Go Into My Prototype?

You've picked the tool to create your MVP and are ready to get started. There is no need to prototype the entire product experience. Instead, simulate the most important part of the experience for your customer and your business. Focus on the core workflows that illustrate your MVP.

Focusing on the primary workflows of your MVP gives the team a sense of temporary tunnel vision (in a good way!), allowing them to focus on a specific portion of the experience and assess its validity and efficacy.

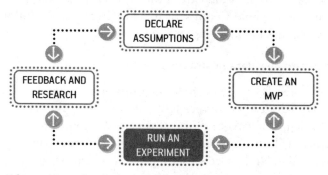

Figure 5-5. *Where prototyping fits in the Lean UX cycle*

Demos and Previews

Test your prototyped MVP with your teammates, stakeholders, and members of other teams. Take it to the lunch area and share it with colleagues who work on different projects. Ensure that people within the company are providing the team with insights into how well it works, how they'll use it, and whether it's worth additional investment. Let stakeholders click through it and give you their insights and thoughts.

Prototypes help show the project's stakeholders that progress is being made. If your team has a demo day (and if it doesn't, it should), bring the prototype there to show progress on the project. The more exposure the MVP gets, the more insight you'll have as to its validity. Next, take your prototype to customers and potential customers. Let them click through the experience and collect their feedback.

Putting It All Together: Using a Prototype MVP

Here's how one team I worked with recently used a prototype MVP. In this case study, the team was considering making a significant change to their offering. We used a prototype MVP to support the research and decision-making process.

This established startup was struggling with their current product—an exclusive subscription-based community for group collaboration. It had been in market for a few years and had gained traction, but adoption had reached a plateau—new users were not signing up. Realizing that a radical change was in order, especially in light of growing competition, they were considering revamping their business model and opening up the product to a significantly broader market segment. Their concern was twofold:

- Would current users accept this change, given that it would alter the exclusive nature of the community?

- Would the new market segment even be interested in this type of product?

The team was worried that they could take a double hit. They feared that existing users would abandon the product and that there wouldn't be enough new users coming on board to make up for the shortfall.

I worked with the team to define our plan as a hypothesis. We laid out the new market segment and defined the core set of functionality we wanted to provide to that segment. It was only a subset of the ultimate vision, but it could be articulated in five wireframes.

We spent a week creating the wireframes using Balsamiq to ensure that our developers, marketers, and executives were on board with the new direction. We showed the wireframes to current customers (twice!) over the course of these five days and ended up with a clickable prototype—our MVP.

The timing for our experiment was fortuitous: there was a conference full of potential customers scheduled for the following week in Texas. The team flew down to the conference and walked the halls of the convention center with the prototype on our iPads.

The mockups worked great on the iPads: customers tapped, swiped, and chatted with us about the new offering. Three days later, we returned to NYC with feedback written on every sticky note and scrap of paper available.

We gathered the notes into groups, and some clear themes emerged. Customer feedback made us realize that although there was merit to this new business plan, we would need further differentiation from existing products in the marketplace if we were going to succeed.

All told, we spent eight business days developing our hypotheses, creating our MVP, and getting market feedback. This work put us in a great position to refine the product to fit our market segment more effectively.

Non-prototype MVPs

For many teams, the default approach to creating an MVP is to create a prototype—to immediately begin designing and writing code. It's easy to understand this approach: we are trained to test our designs and our code, so when we think about validation, we naturally think about creating a product mockup to test. There are many occasions when this step isn't necessary and can even be harmful, though. As valuable as prototyping is, it isn't the only way forward.

Sometimes it makes sense to create an MVP that doesn't simulate your product and instead lets you test something related to your product. For example, when your team is trying to determine the value of a new feature or product, it often makes sense to use a non-prototype MVP to learn whether you're on the right path.

The mantra to keep in mind when creating non-prototype MVPs is this: *you can always go leaner.* To plan your MVP, ask yourself the following questions:

1. What am I trying to learn?

2. What are the main signals I need from the market to validate my hypothesis?

3. Are there any other signals I can test for that will serve as indicators for my main signal?

4. What's the fastest way for me to find this information?

As an example, let's answer these questions for a solution that an ecommerce company wants to test:

1. *What am I trying to learn?* We are trying to learn whether this new ecommerce solution will increase purchases.

2. *What are the main signals I need from the market to validate my hypothesis?* The main signal we're seeking from the market is an increase in completed purchases.

3. *Are there any signals I can test for that will serve as indicators for my main signal?* Instead of completed purchases, can we test for customer intent and use that as a proxy for purchases?

4. *What's the fastest way for me to find this information?* Let's send out an email to a subset of our users offering a few items for sale and count click-throughs for that call-to-action. This will help us determine interest and intent to purchase.

Types of Non-Prototype MVPs

Let's take a quick look at some techniques for creating non-protoype MVPs.

Email

> Email is a very powerful tool when it comes to learning about your customers. Open rates, click-throughs, and task completion rates for recipients all provide insight into whether your idea has value.

Google Ad Words

> A very inexpensive experiment to run is to purchase Google Ad Words advertisements that target searches relevant to your business. By monitoring what people are searching for, you'll start to get feedback on what kind of language resonates with your audience. By measuring click-throughs, you can see how much interest there is in the words and messages you propose.

Landing Page

> A landing page for click-through traffic from Google ads can further validate your thinking. A landing page is the online equivalent of a Wild West movie studio set. It's just a facade of your service, built with a very specific and obvious call-to-action on it. Whether it's Sign-up, Buy Now, or Share-With-A-Friend, every user who completes the task on your landing page counts as validation of your product idea.

The button to nowhere

> A feature can be tested on your site by adding a button to the interface that touts the new functionality. That button does nothing more than measure the number of times it's clicked. Each click indicates a customer's desire for that feature. With enough measurable interest, further development of the feature can continue. Of course, you should give the user some explanation of why the feature isn't working. You can use this further interaction as a chance to capture an email address or another bit of feedback.

Hybrids and Creativity

When I talk to teams and entrepreneurs, I'm often impressed by how creative they can be in their approach to creating MVPs. Designing tests is a creative process, and you should use the methods listed in this chapter as inspiration for your creativity. The best approach for you will often be a mashup of many approaches.

Here's an example of how Cheryl Yeoh launched CityPockets using a hybrid approach called a Concierge MVP to find out whether her idea solved a real problem and if there was enough demand to justify building it for real.

Cheryl Yeoh started CityPockets from the hypothesis that people had trouble managing, keeping track of, and redeeming all the daily deals and coupons they purchased online. She interviewed customers to validate that indeed there was a need, but she wasn't sure if her solution—an online wallet for all of these coupons—would bring the kind of value these customers needed. To validate her hypothesis, she launched an MVP version of CityPockets.com that featured only a front end. Building the back-end processing and integration she would need was going to be costly; she didn't want to spend her money unless she was sure her customers would find her service valuable.

Instead of building a back end, Cheryl assigned a unique email address to each customer who signed up for the service. She instructed her customers to forward all of their coupon emails to that address. Behind the scenes, Cheryl was manually entering every coupon into a database. She set an arbitrary target outcome for herself: 500 emails a day. If customers were sending her 500 emails a day, she felt confident concluding there would be enough demand for the service to merit further investment. She would be ready at that point to build a back end to take over the processing.

This approach—though it involved some design and coding—left out the heavy lifting. Instead, it let Cheryl focus her investment on the smallest possible set of features she needed to support her learning. At the end of the day, this is the essence of the Lean UX approach. Design only what you need. Deliver it quickly. Create enough customer contact to get meaningful feedback fast.

Conclusion

In this chapter, we defined the Minimum Viable Product as the smallest thing you can make to learn whether your hypothesis is valid. In addition, we discussed the various forms an MVP can take, took a closer look at prototyping, and discussed tactics for learning that don't require building prototypes.

In Chapter 6, we take a look at various types of research you can use to make sure that your designs are hitting the mark. We also take a look at how your team can make sense of all the feedback your research will generate.

CHAPTER 6

Feedback and Research

*Research is formalized curiosity. It is poking and
prying with a purpose.*

Zora Neale Hurston

It's now time to put our MVP to the test. All of our work up to this point
has been based on assumptions; now we must begin the validation process.
We use lightweight, continuous, and collaborative research techniques to
do this.

Research with users is at the heart of most approaches to UX. Too often,
teams outsource research work to specialized research teams. And too
often, research activities take place only on rare occasions—either at the
beginning of a project or at the end. Lean UX solves the problems these
tactics create by making research both continuous and collaborative. Let's
dig in to see how to do that.

In this chapter, we cover:

- Collaborative research techniques that allow you to build shared
  understanding with your team
- Continuous research techniques that allow you to build small, informal
  qualitative research studies into every iteration

- Which artifacts to test and what results you can expect from each of these tests

- How to incorporate the voice of the customer throughout the Lean UX cycle

- How to use A/B testing (described later in this chapter) in your research

- How to reconcile contradictory feedback from multiple sources

Continuous and Collaborative

Lean UX takes basic UX research techniques and overlays two important ideas. First, Lean UX research is continuous; this means that you build research activities into every sprint. Instead of a costly and disruptive big bang process, we make research bite-sized so that we can fit it into our ongoing process. Second, Lean UX research is collaborative: you don't rely on the work of specialized researchers to deliver learning to your team. Instead, research activities and responsibilities are distributed and shared across the entire team. By eliminating the handoff between researchers and team members, we increase the quality of our learning. Our goal in all of this is to create a rich shared understanding across the team. See Figure 6-1.

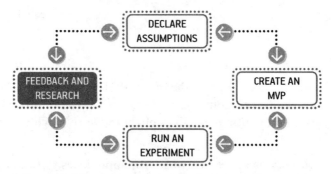

Figure 6-1. *Collecting feedback via research is the final step in the Lean UX cycle.*

Collaborative Discovery

Collaborative design (covered in Chapter 4) is one of two main ways to bridge functions within a Lean UX team. *Collaborative discovery*— working as a team to test ideas in the market—is the other. Collaborative discovery is an approach to research that gets the entire team out of the building—literally and figuratively—to meet with and learn from customers. It gives everyone on the team a chance to see how the hypotheses are testing and, most importantly, multiplies the number of inputs the team can use to gather customer insight.

It's essential that you and your team conduct research together; that's why I call it *collaborative* discovery. Outsourcing this task dramatically reduces its value: it wastes time, it squanders team-building, and it filters the information through deliverables, handoffs, and interpretation. Don't do it.

Researchers sometimes object to this approach to research. As trained professionals, they are right to point out that they have special knowledge that is important to the research process. I agree. That's why you should include a researcher on your team if you can. Just don't outsource the work to that person. Instead, use the researcher as a coach to help your team plan and execute your activities.

Collaborative discovery in the field

Collaborative discovery is a way to get out into the field with your team. Here's how you do it:

- As a team, review your questions, assumptions, hypotheses, and MVPs. Decide as a team what you need to learn.

- Working as a team, decide whom you'll need to speak to in order to address your learning goals.

- Create an interview guide (see the following sidebar) that you can all use to guide your conversations.

- Break your team into interview pairs, mixing up the various roles and disciplines within each pair (i.e., try not to have designers paired with designers).

- Arm each pair with a version of the MVP.

- Send each team out to meet with customers/users.

- Have one team member conduct interviews while the other takes notes.

- Start with questions, conversations, and observations.

- Demonstrate the MVP later in the session and allow the customer to interact with it.

- Collect notes as the customer provides feedback.

- When the lead interviewer is done, switch roles to give the note-taker a chance to ask follow-up questions.

- At the end of the interview, ask the customer for referrals to other people who might also provide useful feedback.

Collaborative discovery: an example

A team I worked with at PayPal set out with an Axure prototype to conduct a collaborative discovery session. The team was made up of two designers, a UX researcher, four developers, and a product manager; they split into teams of two and three. Each developer was paired with a nondeveloper. Before setting out, the team brainstormed what they'd like to learn from their prototype and used the outcome of that session to write brief interview guides. Their product was targeted at a broad consumer market, so they decided to head out to the shopping malls near their office. Each pair targeted a different mall. They spent two hours in the field stopping strangers, asking them questions, and demonstrating their prototypes. To build up their skillset, they changed roles (from lead interviewer to note taker) an hour into their research.

When they reconvened, each pair read their notes to the rest of the team. Almost immediately, they began to see patterns emerge, proving some of their assumptions and disproving others. Using this new information, they adjusted the design of their prototype and headed out again later that afternoon. After a full day of field research, it was clear which ideas had legs and which needed pruning. When they began the next sprint the following day, every member of the team was working from the same baseline of clarity, having established a shared understanding by means of collaborative discovery the day before.

Continuous Discovery

A critical best practice in Lean UX is building a regular cadence of customer involvement. Regularly scheduled conversations with customers minimize the time between hypothesis creation, experiment design, and user feedback, allowing you to validate your hypotheses quickly. In general, knowing you're never more than a few days away from customer feedback has a powerful effect on teams. It takes the pressure away from your decision making because you know that you're never more than a few days from getting meaningful data from the market.

Continuous discovery in the lab: three users every Thursday

Although you can create a standing schedule of fieldwork based on the techniques described in this chapter, it's much easier to bring customers into the building—you just need to be a little creative in order to get the whole team involved.

I like to use a weekly rhythm to bring customers into the building to participate in research. I call this "3-12-1," because it's based on the following guidelines: three users, by 12 noon, once a week (Figure 6-2).

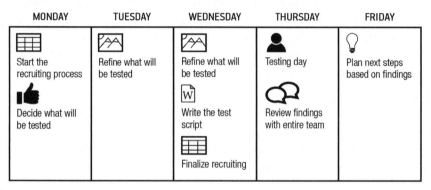

Figure 6-2. *The 3-12-1 activity calendar.*

Here's how the team's activities break down:

Monday: Recruiting and planning

> Decide, as a team, what will be tested this week. Decide who you need to recruit for tests and start the recruiting process. Outsource this job if at all possible; it's very time-consuming.

Tuesday: Refining the components of the test

> Based on the stage your MVP is in, start refining the design, the prototype, or the product to a point that will allow you to tell at least one complete story when your customers see it.

Wednesday: Continue refining, writing the script, and finalizing recruiting

> Put the final touches on your MVP. Write the test script that your moderator will follow with each participant. (Your moderator should be someone on the team, if at all possible.) Finalize the recruiting and schedule for Thursday's tests.

Thursday: Testing!

Spend the morning testing your MVP with customers. Spend no more than an hour with each customer. Everyone on the team should take notes. The team should plan to watch from a separate location. Review the findings with the entire project team immediately after the last participant is done.

Friday: Planning

Use your new insight to decide whether your hypotheses were validated and what you need to do next.

Simplify Your Test Environment

Many firms have established usability labs in house; it used to be that you needed one. These days, you don't need a lab—all you need is a quiet place in your office and a computer with a network connection and a webcam. One specialized tool I recommend is desktop recording and broadcasting software such as Morae, Silverback, or GoToMeeting.

The broadcasting software is a key element. It allows you to bring the test sessions to team members and stakeholders who can't be present. This method has an enormous impact on collaboration because it spreads understanding of your customers deep into your organization. It's hard to overstate how powerful this approach is.

Who Should Watch?

The short answer is: your whole team. Like almost every other aspect of Lean UX, usability testing should be a group activity. With the entire team watching the tests, absorbing the feedback, and reacting in real time, you'll need fewer subsequent debriefings. The team will learn firsthand where their efforts are succeeding and failing. Nothing is more humbling (and motivating) than seeing a user struggle with the software you just built.

A Word about Recruiting Participants

Recruiting, scheduling, and confirming participants is time-intensive. Prevent this additional overhead by offloading the work to a third-party recruiter. The recruiter does the work and gets paid for each participant he or she brings in. In addition, the recruiter takes care of the screening, scheduling, and replacement of no-shows on testing day. These recruiters can cost anywhere from $75 to $150 per participant recruited.

Case Study: Three Users Every Thursday at Meetup

One company that has taken the concept of "three users every Thursday" to a new level is Meetup. Based in New York and under the guidance of VP of Product, Strategy, and Community Andres Glusman, Meetup started with a desire to test each and every one of their new features and products.

After pricing some outsourced options, they decided to keep things in house and take an iterative approach in their search for what they called their "minimally viable process." Initially, they tried to test with the user, moderator, and team all in the same room. They got some decent results from this approach— and there was lots to learn from this technique, including that it can be scaled—but found that the test participants would get a bit freaked out with so many folks in the room.

Over time, they evolved to having the testing in one room with only the moderator joining the user. The rest of the team would watch the video feed from a separate conference room (Meetup originally used Morae to share the video; today they are using GoToMeeting).

Meetup doesn't write testing scripts because they're not sure what will be tested each day. Instead, product managers interact with test moderators, using instant messaging to help guide the conversations with users. The team debriefs immediately after the tests are complete and is able to move forward quickly.

Meetup recruited directly from the Meetup community from day one. For participants outside of their community, the team used a third-party recruiter. Ultimately, they decided to bring this responsibility in-house, assigning the work to the dedicated researcher they'd hired to handle all testing.

The team scaled up from three users once a week to testing every day except Monday. Their core objective was to minimize the time between concept and customer feedback.

Meetup's practical minimum viable process orientation can also be seen in their approach to mobile testing. As their mobile usage numbers grew, Meetup didn't want to delay testing on mobile platforms while waiting for fancy mobile testing equipment. Instead, they built their own—for $28 (see Figure 6-3).

Figure 6-3. *Meetup's mobile usability testing rig.*

As of 2012, Meetup has successfully scaled their minimum viable usability testing process to an impressive program. They run approximately 600 test sessions per year at a total cost of about $30,000 (not including staffing costs). This cost includes 100 percent video and notes coverage for every session. When you consider that this is roughly equivalent to the cost of running one major outsourced usability study, this achievement is truly amazing.

Making Sense of the Research—A Team Activity

Whether your team does fieldwork or lab work, research generates a lot of raw data. Making sense of this data can be time-consuming and frustrating, so the process is often handed over to specialists who are asked to synthesize research findings. You shouldn't do things this way. Instead, work as hard as you can to make sense of the data as a team.

As soon as possible after the research sessions are over—preferably the same day, or at least the following day—gather the team together for a review session. When the team has reassembled, ask everyone to read their findings to each other. An efficient way to do this is to transcribe the notes people read out loud onto index cards or sticky notes, then sort the notes into themes. This process of reading, grouping, and discussing gets everyone's input out on the table and builds the shared understanding that you seek. With themes identified, you and your team can then determine next steps for your MVP.

Confusion, Contradiction, and (Lack of) Clarity

As you and your team collect feedback from various sources and try to synthesize your findings, you will inevitably come across situations in which your data presents you with contradictions. How do you make sense of it all? Here are a couple of ways to maintain your momentum and ensure that you're maximizing your learning:

Look for patterns

> As you review the research, keep an eye out for patterns in the data. These patterns reveal multiple instances of user opinion that represent elements to explore. If something doesn't fall into a pattern, it is likely an outlier.

Park your outliers

> As tempting as it is to ignore outliers (or try to serve them in your solution), don't do it. Instead, create a parking lot or backlog for them. As your research progresses over time (remember, you're doing this every week), you may discover other outliers that match the pattern. Be patient.

Verify with other sources

> If you're not convinced that the feedback you're seeing through one channel is valid, look for it in other channels. Are the customer support emails reflecting the same concerns as your usability studies? Is the value of your prototype echoed by customers both inside and outside your office? If not, your sample may have been disproportionately skewed.

Identifying Patterns over Time

Most UX research programs are structured to get a conclusive answer. Typically, you will plan to do enough research to definitively answer a question or set of questions. Lean UX research puts a priority on being continuous, which means that you're structuring your research activities very differently. Instead of running big studies, you'll see a small number of users every week. Therefore, some questions may remain open over a couple of weeks. Another result is that interesting patterns can reveal themselves over time.

For example, our regular test sessions at TheLadders revealed an interesting change in our customers' attitudes over time. In 2008, when we first started meeting with job seekers on a regular basis, we would discuss various ways to communicate with employers. One of the options we proposed was SMS. Because our audience was typically made up of high-income earners in their late forties and early fifties, their early responses showed a strong disdain for SMS as a legitimate communication method. To them, it was something their kids did (and that perhaps they did with their kids), but it was certainly not a "proper" way to conduct a job search.

By 2011, though, SMS messages had taken off in the United States. As text messaging gained acceptance in business culture, this attitude began to soften. Week after week, as we sat with job seekers, we began to see these opinions change. We saw job seekers become far more likely to use SMS in a mid-career job search than they would have been just a few years before.

We would never have recognized this as an audience-wide trend had we not been speaking with a sample of that audience week in and week out. As part of our regular interaction with customers, we always asked a regular set of level-setting questions to capture the "vital signs" of the job seeker's search, no matter what other questions, features, or products we were testing. Anecdotally, these findings would not have swayed our beliefs about our target audience. Aggregated over time, they became very powerful and shaped our future product discussions and considerations.

Test Everything

In order to maintain a regular cadence of user testing, your team must adopt a "test everything" policy. Whatever is ready on testing day is what goes in front of the users. This policy liberates your team from rushing toward testing day deadlines. Instead, you'll find yourself taking advantage of your weekly test sessions to get insight at every stage of design and development. You must, however, set expectations properly for the type of feedback you'll be able to generate with each type of artifact.

Sketches

Feedback collected on sketches (Figure 6-4) helps you validate the value of your concept. What you *won't* get at this level is tactical, step-by-step feedback on the process, insight about design elements, or even meaningful feedback on copy choices. You won't be able to learn much (if anything) about the usability of your concept.

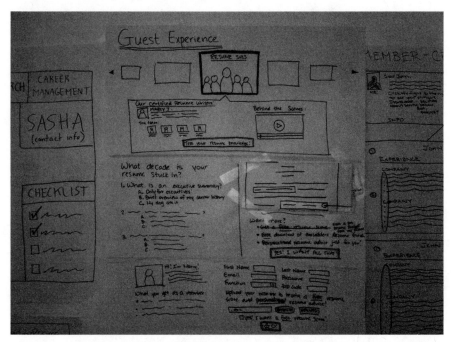

Figure 6-4. *Example of a sketch that can be used with customers.*

Static Wireframes

Showing test participants wireframes (Figure 6-5) lets you assess the information hierarchy and layout of your experience. In addition, you'll get feedback on taxonomy, navigation, and information architecture.

You'll receive the first trickles of workflow feedback, but at this point your test participants are focused primarily on the words on the page and the selections they're making. Wireframes provide a good opportunity to start testing copy choices.

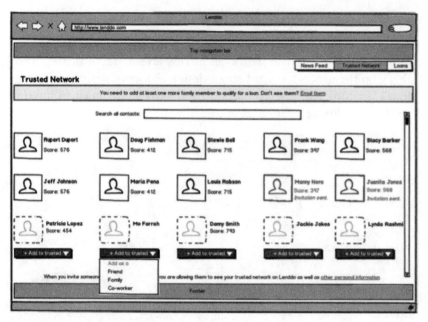

Figure 6-5. *Example of a wireframe.*

High-Fidelity Visual Mockups (Not Clickable)

Moving into high-fidelity visual-design assets, you receive much more tactical feedback. Test participants will be able to respond to branding, aesthetics, and visual hierarchy, as well as aspects of figure/ground relationships, grouping of elements, and the clarity of your calls-to-action. Your test participants will also (almost certainly) weigh in on the effectiveness of your color palette.

Nonclickable mockups still don't let your customers react naturally to the design or subsequent steps in the experience. Instead of asking your customers how they feel about the outcome of each click, you have to ask them what they would expect and then validate those responses against your planned experience.

Mockups (Clickable)

A set of clickable mockups—essentially a prototype created in Axure, Fireworks, ProtoShare or any other viable prototyping tool (see Figure 6-6)— avoids the pitfalls of showing screens that don't link together. Users see the actual results of their clicks. This type of mockup will not allow you to assess interactions with data (so you can't test search performance, for example), but you can still learn a lot about the structure of your product.

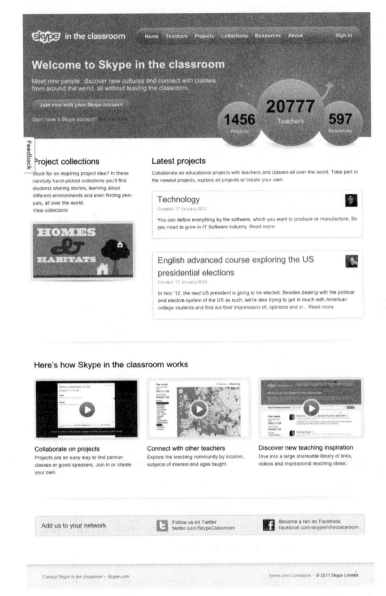

Figure 6-6. *Example of clickable mockup from Skype in the Classroom. (Design by Made By Many.)*

Coded Prototypes

Live code is the best experience you can put in front of your test participants. It replicates the design, behavior, and workflow of your product. The feedback is real, and you can apply it directly to the experience. You may simulate a live-data connection or actually connect to live data; if you design your test experience well, users won't be able to tell, but their reactions will provide you with direct insight into the way real data affects the experience (Figure 6-7).

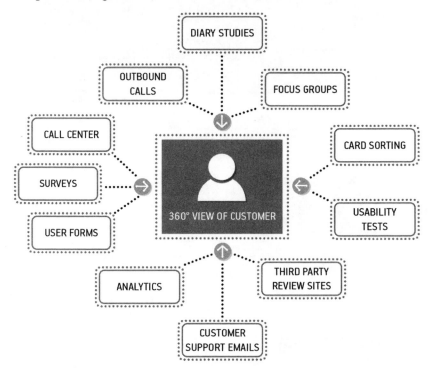

Figure 6-7. *Customers can provide feedback through many channels.*

Monitoring Techniques for Continuous, Collaborative Discovery

In the previous discussions in this chapter, I looked at ways to use qualitative research on a regular basis to evaluate your hypotheses. But once you launch your product or feature, your customers will start giving you constant feedback—and not only on your product. They will tell you about themselves, about the market, about the competition. This insight is invaluable, and comes into your organization from every corner. Seek out these treasure troves of customer intelligence within your organization and harness them to drive your ongoing product design and research.

Customer Service

Customer support agents talk to more customers on a daily basis than you will over the course of an entire project. There are multiple ways to harness their knowledge:

- Reach out to them and ask them what they're hearing from customers about the sections of the product on which you're working.

- Hold regular monthly meetings with them to understand the trends. What do customers love this month? What do they hate?

- Tap their deep product knowledge to learn how they would solve the challenges your team is working on. Include them in design sessions and design reviews.

- Incorporate your hypotheses into their call scripts—one of the cheapest ways to test your ideas is to suggest it as a fix to customers calling in with a relevant complaint.

In the mid-2000s, I ran the UX team at a medium-sized tech company in Portland, Oregon. One of the ways we prioritized the work was by regularly checking the pulse of the customer base. We did this with a standing monthly meeting with our customer service reps. Each month, they would provide us with the top 10 things customers were complaining about. We used this information to focus our efforts and to subsequently measure the efficacy of our work. If we attempted to solve one of these pain points, this monthly conversation gave us a clear indication of whether our efforts were bearing fruit; if the issue was not receding in the top 10 list, our solution had not worked.

An additional benefit of this effort was that the customer service team realized someone was listening to their insights and began proactively giving us customer feedback outside of our monthly meeting. The dialog that ensued provided us with a continuous feedback loop to use with many of our product hypotheses.

Onsite Feedback Surveys

Set up a feedback mechanism in your product that allows customers to send you their thoughts regularly. A few options include:

- Simple email forms

- Customer support forums

- Third-party community sites

You can repurpose these tools for research by doing things such as:

- Counting how many inbound emails you're getting from a particular section of the site

- Participating in online discussions and suggesting some of your hypotheses

- Soliciting community sites for hard-to-find test participants

These inbound customer feedback channels provide feedback from the point of view of your most active and engaged customers. Here are a few tactics for getting other points of view:

Search logs

Search terms are clear indicators of what customers are seeking on your site. Search patterns indicate what they're finding and what they're not finding. Repeated queries with slight variations show a user's challenge in finding certain information.

One way to use search logs for MVP validation is to launch a test page for the feature you're planning. Following the search logs will tell you if the test content (or feature) on that page is meeting the user's needs. If they continue to search on variations of that content, your experiment has failed.

Site usage analytics

Site usage logs and analytics packages—especially funnel analyses— show how customers are using the site, where they're dropping off, and how they try to manipulate the product to do the things they need or expect it to do. Understanding these reports provides real-world context for the decisions the team needs to make.

In addition, use analytics tools to determine the success of experiments that have launched publicly. How has the experiment shifted usage of the product? Are your efforts achieving the outcome you defined? These tools provide an unbiased answer.

A/B testing

A/B testing is a technique, originally developed by marketers, to gauge which of two (or more) relatively similar concepts achieve a goal more effectively. When applied in the Lean UX framework, A/B testing becomes a powerful tool to determine the validity of your hypotheses. Applying A/B testing is relatively straightforward once your hypotheses evolve into working code.

Here's how it works: take the proposed experience (your hypothesis) and publish it to your audience. However, instead of letting every customer see it, release it only to a small subset of users. Then, measure your success criteria for that audience. Compare it to the other group (your control cohort) and note the differences. Did your new idea move the needle in the right direction? If it did, you've got a winning hypothesis. If not, you've got an audience of customers to pull from and engage directly to understand why their behavior went unchanged.

There are several companies that offer A/B testing suites, but they all basically work the same way. The name suggests that you can only test two things, but in fact you can test as many permutations of your experience as you'd like (this is called A/B/n testing). The trick is to make sure that the changes you're making are small enough that any change in behavior can be attributed to them directly. If you change too many things, any behavioral change cannot be directly attributed to your any one hypothesis.

Companies that offer A/B testing tools include Unbounce for landing page testing, Google Content Experiments (formerly Site Optimizer), Adobe Test&Target (formerly Omniture), and Webtrends Optimize.

Conclusion

In this chapter I covered many ways to start validating the MVPs and experiments you've built around your hypotheses. I looked at continuous discovery and collaborative discovery techniques. I discussed how to build a lean usability-testing process every week and covered what you should test and what to expect from those tests. I also looked at ways to monitor your customer experience in a Lean UX context and touched on the power of A/B testing.

These techniques, used in conjunction with the processes outlined in Chapters 3 through 5, make up the full Lean UX process loop. Your goal is to cycle through this loop as often as possible, refining your thinking with each iteration.

In the next section, I move away from process and take a look at how Lean UX integrates within your organization. Whether you're a startup, a large company, or a digital agency, I'll cover all of the organizational shifts you'll need to make to support the Lean UX approach. These ideas will work in most existing processes, but in Chapter 7, I'll specifically cover how to make Lean UX and Agile software development work well together.

MAKING IT WORK

From 2007 to 2011, I led the UX team at TheLadders, an online job board based in New York City. During my tenure, the company began its transition from Waterfall to Agile. It was a developer-driven effort, but the company recognized that unless UX was included, the transition would fail. It was up to me to figure out how we would integrate Lean UX with this new style of working. In 2007, if you Googled "Agile UX," the results page would be littered with blog posts, articles, and case studies that documented failure and frustration. The main themes seemed to be cries of "Agile sucks!" and screeds claiming "UX has no business working this way."

Undeterred, I continued to search for collaboration and integration ideas. I came across Lynne Miller and Desiree Sy's "staggered sprint" model—in which the UX team works at a sprint ahead of the developers—and gave it a try. Although it was helpful in getting us to think about our work in smaller bursts, it did nothing to increase collaboration between the disciplines or to reduce wasted effort on specs for features that would never be built.

We were convinced there was a better way, so, like good Agilistas, we continued to tune our process. After several months, I felt like we'd hit our stride. We had increased collaboration, started producing fewer documents, and increased our customer validation efforts. The internal cries of "Agile sucks" and "I hate this" had also subsided. I was feeling pretty good about our little team.

One Monday morning I walked into the office ready to start the week and found the diagram in Figure III-1 printed out and placed neatly on my desk.

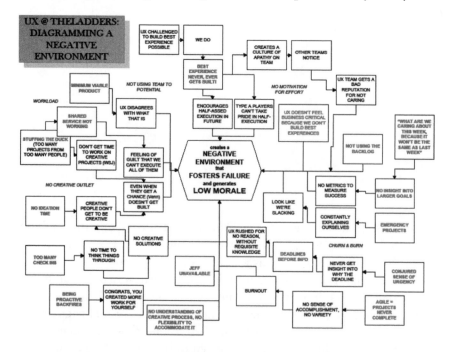

Figure III-1. *The UX team at TheLadders expressed their feelings about our Agile/UX integration efforts.*

It turns out things weren't as rosy as I'd thought. My team had gone off and held their own retrospective (read: venting session) and produced this diagram as their "deliverable" to me. It caught me a bit by surprise, but as I dug into the details of the document and discussed the key pain points with the team, the holes in our process became evident.

Look at the diagram: if you've tried to integrate Agile and UX, perhaps you recognize some of these problems. The team felt there wasn't enough time to do "gold medal" work. They felt their work wasn't mission-critical. They felt that they didn't have time to iterate. The list goes on. When I show this diagram to other teams struggling to integrate Agile and UX, there are always plenty of rueful smiles of recognition.

Finding this diagram on my desk was a humbling experience, but it touched off a dialog and engaged the learning process that is at the heart of Agile approaches. The dialog allowed us to begin a process of discovery that ultimately resulted in the cross-functional collaboration that made our Agile process a success, as described in Section II.

About Section III

How can you integrate the Lean UX process into your organization? That's the question I'll answer in Section III.

In Chapter 7, "Integrating Lean UX and Agile," I'll take the tactics discussed in Section II and show you exactly how they fit into a typical Scrum process and how they make it more effective.

In Chapter 8, "Making Organizational Shifts," I'll dig into the specific organizational changes that need to be made to support this way of working. It's not just software developers and designers who need to find a way to work together. Product managers, project managers—in short, your whole product development engine—is going to need to change if you want to create a truly Agile organization.

Integrating Lean UX and Agile

Agile methods are now mainstream. At the same time, thanks to the huge success of products such as the Kindle and the iPhone, so is user experience design. But making Agile work with UX has long been a challenge. In this chapter, I review how Lean UX methods can fit within the most popular flavor of Agile—the Scrum process—and discuss how blending Lean UX and Agile can create a more productive team and a more collaborative process. I'll cover:

Definition of terms

> Just to make sure we're all on the same page about certain words like "sprint" and "story."

Staggered sprints

> The one-time savior of Agile/UX integration is now just a stepping stone to true team cohesion.

Listening to Scrum's rhythms

> The meeting cadences of Scrum are clear guideposts for Lean UX integration.

Participation

> A truly cross-functional process requires that everyone be a part of it.

Design as a team sport

> Ensuring that the once-closed design process is now open to all team members is key to your success.

Managing up and out

Clear obstacles to your team's progress by being proactive with your communication.

Some Definitions

Agile processes, including Scrum, use many proprietary terms. Over time, many of these terms have taken on a life of their own. To ensure that I'm using them clearly, I've taken the time to define a few of them here (If you're familiar with Scrum, you can skip this section.)

Scrum

An agile methodology promoting time-boxed cycles, team self-organization, and high team accountability. Scrum is the most popular form of Agile.

User story

The smallest unit of work expressed as a benefit to the end user. Typical user stories are written using the following syntax:

As a [user type]

I want to [accomplish something]

So that [some benefit happens]

Backlog

A prioritized list of user stories. The backlog is the most powerful project management tool in Agile. It is through the active grooming of the backlog that the team manages their daily workload and refocuses their efforts based on incoming knowledge. It is how the team stays agile.

Sprint:

A single team cycle. The goal of each sprint is to deliver working software. Most Scrum teams work in two-week sprints.

Stand-up:

A daily short team meeting at which each member addresses the day's challenges—one of Scrum's self-accountability tools. Each member must declare to all teammates, every day, what he or she is doing and what's getting in his or her way.

Retrospective

A meeting at the end of each sprint that takes an honest look at what went well, what went poorly, and how the team will try to improve the process in the next sprint. Your process is as iterative as your product. Retrospectives give your team the chance to optimize your process with every sprint.

Iteration planning meeting

A meeting at the beginning of each sprint at which the team plans the upcoming sprint. Sometimes this meeting includes estimation and story gathering. This is the meeting that determines the initial prioritization of the backlog.

Beyond Staggered Sprints

In May 2007, Desiree Sy and Lynn Miller published "Adapting Usability Investigations for Agile User-centered Design" in the *Journal of Usability Studies* (*http://www.upassoc.org/upa_publications/jus/2007may/agile-ucd.pdf*). Sy and Miller were some of the first people to try to combine Agile and UX, and many of us were excited by the solutions they were proposing. In the article, Sy and Miller describe in detail their idea of a productive integration of Agile and user-centered design. They use a technique called Cycle 0 (you may have heard it called "Sprint Zero" or "Staggered Sprints" as well).

In short, Sy and Miller describe a process in which design activity takes place one sprint ahead of development (Figure 7-1). Work is designed and validated during the "design sprint" and then passed off into the development stream to be implemented during the development sprint.

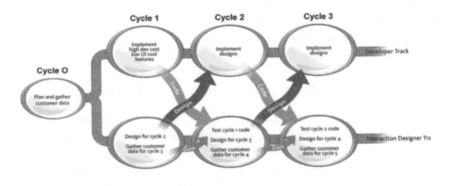

Figure 7-1. *Sy and Miller's "staggered sprints" model.*

Many teams have misinterpreted this model. Sy and Miller always advocated strong collaboration between designers and developers during both the design and development sprints. Many teams have missed this critical point and have instead created workflows in which designers and developers communicate by handoff, creating a kind of mini-waterfall process.

Staggered sprints can work well for some teams. If your development environment does not allow for frequent releases (for example, you work on packaged software, or embedded software, or deliver software to an environment in which continuous deployment is difficult or impossible), the premium on getting the design right is higher. In these cases, Lean UX may not be a great fit for your team, as you'll have to work hard to get the market feedback you need to make many of these techniques work.

For these teams, staggered sprints can allow for more validation of design work—provided that you are still working in a very collaborative manner. And teams transitioning from Waterfall to Agile can benefit from working this way as well, because it teaches you to work in shorter cycles and to divide your work into sequential pieces.

However, this model works best as a transition. It is not where you want your team to end up. Here's why: it becomes very easy to create a situation in which the entire team is never working on the same thing at the same time. You never realize the benefits of cross-functional collaboration because the different disciplines are focused on different things. Without that collaboration, you don't build shared understanding, so you end up relying heavily on documentation and handoffs for communication.

There's another reason this process is less than ideal: it can create unnecessary waste. You waste time creating documentation to describe what happened during the design sprints. And if developers haven't participated in the design sprint, they haven't had a chance to assess the work for feasibility or scope. That conversation doesn't happen until handoff. Can they actually build the specified designs in the next two weeks? If not, the work that went into designing those elements is waste.

Building Lean UX into the Rhythm of Scrum

As I said in the opening to this chapter, we tried using Staggered Sprints at TheLadders. And when we had problems, we continued to improve our process, eventually ending up with a deeply collaborative routine that played out across the rhythms of Scrum. Let's take a look at how you can use Scrum's meeting structure and Lean UX to build an efficient process.

Themes

Scrum has a lot of meetings. Many people frown on meetings, but if you use them as mileposts during your sprint, you can create an integrated Lean UX and Agile process in which the entire team is working on the same thing at the same time.

Let's take a two-week sprint model and assume that we can tie a series of these sprints together under one umbrella, which we'll call a theme (Figure 7-2).

Figure 7-2. *Sprints tied together with a theme.*

Kickoff Sessions for Sketching and Ideation

Each theme should be kicked off with a series of brainstorming and validation exercises like the ones described in Section II. These activities can be as short as an afternoon or as long as a week. You can do them with your immediate team or with a broader group. The scope of the theme will determine how much participation and time these kickoff activities require. The point of this kickoff is to get the entire team sketching and ideating together, creating a backlog of ideas to test and learn from.

Once you've started your sprints, these ideas will be tested, validated, and developed new knowledge will come in, and you'll need to decide what to do with it. You make these decisions by running subsequent shorter brainstorming sessions that take place before each new sprint begins, which allows the team to use the latest insight to create the backlog for the next sprint. See Figure 7-3.

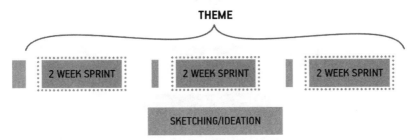

Figure 7-3. *Timing and scope of sketching, ideation, and brainstorming sessions.*

Iteration Planning Meeting

The output of the kickoff session should be brought to the *iteration planning meeting* (IPM). Your mess of sticky notes, sketches, wireframes, paper prototypes, and any other artifacts may seem useless to outside observers but will be meaningful to your team. You made these artifacts together and because of that, you have the shared understanding necessary to extract stories from them. Use them in your IPM (Figure 7-4) to write user stories together, then evaluate and prioritize the stories.

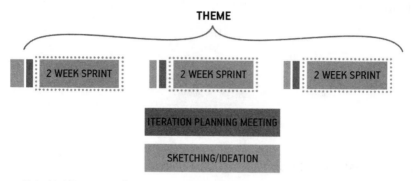

Figure 7-4. *Hold iteration planning meetings immediately after brainstorming sessions.*

User Validation Schedule

Finally, to ensure a constant stream of customer voices to validate against, plan user sessions every single week (Figure 7-5). Your team will never be more than five business days away from customer validation but still your ideas will have ample time to react prior to the end of the sprint. Use the artifacts you created in the ideation sessions as the base material for your user tests. Remember that when the ideas are raw, you are testing for value (i.e., do people want to use my product?). Once you have established a desire for your product, subsequent tests with higher fidelity artifacts will reveal whether your solution is usable.

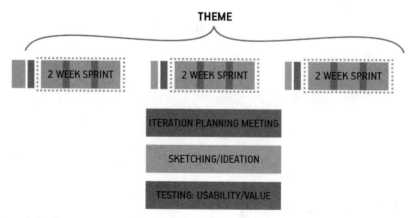

Figure 7-5. *Conversations with users happen every week.*

Participation

One of the big lessons I took away from the diagram I showed at the beginning of Section III was that designers need time to be creative. Two-week cycles of concurrent development and design offer few opportunities for creative time. Some Agile methods take a more flexible approach to time than Scrum does. (For example, Kanban does away with the notion of a two-week batch of work and places the emphasis on single-piece flow.) But you can still make time within a Scrum sprint in which creative activities can take place.

The reason my UX team at TheLadders wasn't finding that time was that we weren't fully participating in the Scrum process. This was not entirely our fault: the content of many Scrum meetings offered little value to UX designers. However, without our participation, our concerns and needs were not taken into account in project plans. As a result, we weren't creating the time within sprints for creative work to take place—the rest of the team didn't understand that this time was needed.

For Lean UX to work in Agile, the entire team must participate in all activities—standups, retrospectives, IPMs, brainstorming sessions—they all require everyone's attendance to be successful. Besides negotiating the complexity of certain features, cross-functional participation allows designers and developers to create effective backlog prioritization.

For example, imagine at the start of a sprint that the first story a team prioritizes has a heavy design component to it. Imagine that the designer wasn't there to voice his or her concern. That team will fail as soon as it meets for its standup the next day. The designer will announce that the story has not been designed. And he or she will say that it will take at least two or three days to complete the design before the story is ready for development. Imagine instead that the designer had participated in the prioritization of the backlog. His or her concern would have been raised at planning time. The team could have selected a story card that needed less design preparation to work on first, which would have bought the designer the time necessary to complete the work.

The other casualty of sparse participation is shared understanding. Teams make decisions in meetings. Those decisions are based on discussions. Even if 90 percent of a meeting is not relevant to your immediate need, the 10 percent that is relevant will save hours of time downstream explaining what happened at the meeting and why certain decisions were made.

Participation allows you to negotiate for the time you need to do your work. This is true for UX designers as much as it is for everyone else on the team.

Design Is a Team Sport: Knowsy Case Study

In this case study, designer and coach Lane Halley details how she brought to the table all the players—development, design, marketing, and stakeholders—to create a tablet game.

In my work as a product designer, I use Lean UX practices on a variety of projects. Recently I've worked on entertainment, ecommerce, and social media products for different platforms, including iPad, iPhone, and Web. The teams have been small, ranging from three to seven people. Most of my projects also share the following characteristics:

- The project is run within an Agile framework (focus on the customer, continuous delivery, team sits together, lightweight documentation, team ownership of decisions, shared rituals like standups, retrospectives, etc.).

- The team contains people with a mix of skills (front- and back-end development, user experience and information architecture, product management and marketing, graphic design, copywriting).

- The people on the team generally performed in their area of expertise/strength but were supportive of other specialties and interested in learning new skills.

Most of the teams I work with create entirely new products or services. They are not working within an existing product framework or structure. In "green fields" projects like these, we are simultaneously trying to discover how this new product or service will be used, how it will behave and how we are going to build it. It's an environment of continual change, and there isn't a lot of time or patience for planning or up-front design.

The Innovation Games Company

The Innovation Games Company (TIGC) produces serious games—online and in-person—for market research. TIGC helps organizations get actionable insights into customer needs and preferences to improve performance through collaborative play. In 2010, I was invited to help TIGC create a new game for the consumer market.

I was part of the team that created Knowsy for iPad, a pass-and-play game that's all about learning what you know about your friends, family, and coworkers, while simultaneously testing how well they know you. The person who knows the other players best wins the game. It is a fast, fun, and truly "social" game for up to six players.

It was our first iPad application, and we had an ambitious deadline: one month to create the game and have it accepted to the App Store. Our small team had a combination of subject-matter expertise and skills in front- and back-end development as well as visual and interaction design. We also asked other people to help us play-test the game at various stages of development.

A Shared Vision Empowers Independent Work

Until a new product is coded, it's hard for people to work within the same product vision. You can recognize a lack of shared vision when the team argues about what features are important or what should be done first. There can also be a general sense that the team is not "moving fast enough," or that the team is going back over the same issues again and again.

While working on Knowsy, I looked for ways that I could make my UX practice more collaborative, visual, lightweight, and iterative. I looked for opportunities to work in real time with other people on the team (such as developers and the product manager) and rough things out as quickly as possible at the lowest responsible level of fidelity.

As we found the right solutions and the team understood and bought into the design concept, I was able to increase fidelity of the design artifacts, confident that we shared a product vision (Figure 7-6).

Figure 7-6. *The Knowsy team with the wall of artifacts behind them.*

Breaking the Design Bottleneck

Early in the project, I sat with the front-end developer to talk about the game design. We created a high-level game flow together on paper, passing the marker back and forth as we talked. This was my opportunity to listen and learn what he was thinking. As we sketched, I was able to point out inconsistencies by asking questions such as, "What do we do when this happens?" This approach had the benefit of changing the dialog from "I'm right and you're wrong" to "How do we solve this problem?"

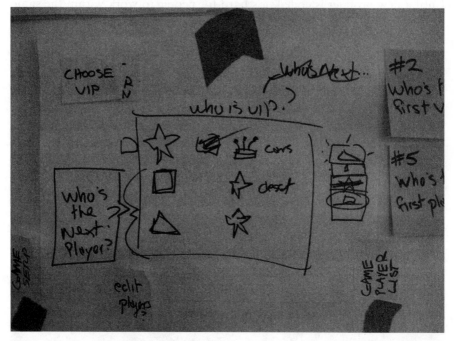

Figure 7-7. *The paper prototype begins to take shape.*

After we had this basic agreement, I was able to create a paper prototype (Figure 7-7) of the game based on the flow and play-test it with the team. The effect on the team was immediate. Suddenly everyone "got it" and was excited about what we were doing. People started to contribute ideas that fit together well, and we were able to identify which parts we could each work on that supported the whole.

Once we were all on the same page, it was easier for me to take some time away from the team and document what we'd agreed in a clickable prototype. See Figure 7-8.

Figure 7-8. *Lane updating the prototype and artifact wall in real time.*

The Outcome

Knowsy's foray into Lean UX proved a success. We got the app to the Apple store by the deadline. I was called back later to help the team do another variant of the product. For that round, I used a similar process. Because I was working remotely and the dev team was not as available to collaborate, I had to make heavier deliverables. Nevertheless, the basic principle of iterating our way to higher fidelity continued.

Beyond the Scrum Team

Management check-ins are one of the biggest obstacles to maintaining team momentum. Designers are used to doing design reviews, but unfortunately, check-ins don't end there. Product owners, stakeholders, CEOs, and clients all want to know how things are going. They all want to bless the project plan going forward. The challenge for outcome-focused teams is that their project plans are dependent on what they are learning. They are responsive, so their typical plan lays out only small batches of work at a time. At most, these teams plan an iteration or two ahead. This perceived "short-sightedness" tends not to satisfy most high-level managers. How then do you keep the check-ins at bay while maintaining the pace of your Lean UX and Scrum processes?

Two words: proactive communication.

I once managed a team that radically altered the workflow for an existing product that had thousands of paying customers. We were so excited by the changes we'd made that we went ahead with the launch without alerting anyone else in the organization. Within an hour of the new product going live, the VP of Customer Service was at my desk, fuming and demanding to know why she wasn't told about this change. Turns out that when customers have problems with the product, they call in for help. Call center reps use scripts to troubleshoot the customers' needs and offer solutions, and they didn't have a script for this new product...because they didn't know it was going to change.

This healthy slice of humble pie served as a valuable lesson. If you want your stakeholders—both those managing you and those dependent on you—to stay out of your way, make sure they are aware of your plans. Here are a few tips:

- Proactively reach out to your product owners and executives.

- Let them know:
  - How the project is going
  - What you tried so far and learned
  - What you'll be trying next

- Keep the conversations focused on outcomes (how you're trending towards your goal), not feature sets.

- Ensure that dependent departments (customer service, marketing, ops, etc.) are aware of upcoming changes that can affect their work.

- Provide them with plenty of time to update their workflows if necessary.

Conclusion

This chapter took a closer look at how Lean UX fits into a Scrum process. In addition, I talked about how cross-functional collaboration allows a team to move forward at a brisk pace and how to handle those pesky stakeholders and managers who always want to know what's going on. I discussed why having everyone participate in all activities is critical and why the staggered sprint model is only a way-point on the path to true agility.

In the next and final chapter, we'll take a look at the organizational shifts that need to be made to support Lean UX. This chapter can serve as a primer for managers on what they'll need to do to set teams up for success.

Making Organizational Shifts

Earlier in this book, I discussed the principles behind Lean UX. I hope you understand from that section that Lean UX is a mindset. I've also discussed some of the key methods of Lean UX, because Lean UX is also a process. As I've worked with clients and taught these methods to teams, it's become clear that Lean UX is also a management method. For this reason, you'll need to make some changes in your organization in order to get the most benefit from working this way.

When I train teams, they sometimes ask me, "How can I put these methods into practice here?" On this point, I'm a little hesitant. Although I'm confident that most organizations can solve these problems, I'm also aware that every organization is different. Finding the right solution is going to require a lot of close work and collaboration with your colleagues.

To prepare you for that work, I'm going to use this chapter to share with you some of the shifts that organizations need to make in order to embrace Lean UX. I'm not going to tell you how to make those shifts. That's your job. But I hope this discussion will help you survey the landscape to find the areas that you're going to address.

In this chapter, we'll discuss the following changes your organization may need to make in these areas:

- Shifting from output to outcomes
- Moving from limited roles to collaborative capabilities
- Embracing new skills

- Creating cross-functional teams

- Creating small teams

- Creating open, collaborative workspaces

- Not relying on heroes

- Eliminating "Big Design Up Front"

- Placing speed first, aesthetics second

- Valuing problem solving

- Embracing UX debt

- Shifting agency culture

- Working with third-party vendors

- Navigating documentation standards

- Being realistic about your environment

- Managing up and out

SHIFT: Outcomes

In Chapter 3, I discussed the role of outcomes in Lean UX. Lean UX teams measure their success not in terms of features completed but in terms of progress toward specific outcomes. Determining outcomes is a leadership activity, one that many organizations are not good at or don't do at all. Too often, leadership directs the product team through a product roadmap—a set of outputs and features that they require the product team to produce

Teams attempting to use Lean UX must be empowered to design the solutions to the business problems with which they are tasked. In other words, they must be empowered to decide for themselves which features will create the outcomes their organizations require. To do this, teams must shift their conversation with leadership from one based on features to one centered on outcomes, and this conversational shift is a radical one. Product managers and product owners must determine which business metrics require the most attention. In turn, they must have conversations around outcomes with their managers. In this way, the shift will inevitably go to the highest levels of the organization.

Leadership must set this direction, and teams must demand this shift from leadership. Managers have to be retrained to give their teams the latitude to experiment. Product requirements conversations must then be grounded in business outcomes: what are we trying to achieve by building this product? This rule holds true for design decisions as well. Success criteria must be redefined and roadmaps must be done away with. In their place, teams build backlogs of hypotheses they'd like to test and prioritize them based on risk, feasibility, and potential success.

SHIFT: Roles

In most companies, the work you do is determined by your job title. That job title comes with a job description. Too often, people in organizations discourage others from working outside the confines of their job descriptions (e.g., "You're not a developer, what can you possibly know about JavaScript?"). This approach is deeply anticollaborative and means that workers' full range of skills, talents, and competencies are unused.

Discouraging cross-functional input encourages organizational silos. The more discrete a person's job is, the easier it becomes to retreat to the safe confines of that discipline. As a result, conversation across disciplines wanes and mistrust, finger-pointing, and "cover your ass" (CYA) behavior grows. Silos are the death of collaborative teams.

For Lean UX to succeed, your organization needs to adopt a mantra of "competencies over roles." Every team member possesses a core competency—design, software development, research, etc.—and must deliver on that skill set. However, he or she may also possess secondary competencies that make the team work more efficiently.

Allow your colleagues to contribute in any disciplines in which they have expertise and interest. You'll find that working this way creates a more engaged team that can complete tasks more efficiently. You'll also find that it builds camaraderie across job titles, as people with different disciplines show interest in what their colleagues are doing. Teams that enjoy working together produce better work.

SHIFT: New Skills for UX Designers

Many companies hire designers to create wireframes, specs, and site maps. This hiring is done to fill the "design" phase of the waterfall process. Plugging interaction designers into these existing workflows limits their effectiveness by limiting the scope of their work, which has a side effect of reinforcing a siloed team model.

The success of a collaborative team demands more. Although teams still need core UX skills, designers must add facilitation as one of their core competencies. This change requires two significant shifts to the way we've worked to date:

Designers must open up the design process.

The team—not the individual—must own the product design. Instead of hiding behind a monitor for days at a time, designers must bring teams into the design process, seek their input, and build that insight into the design. Doing so will begin to break down silos and allow a more cross-functional conversation to take place.

Designers must take a leadership role on their team.

Your colleagues are used to critiquing your design work. What they're not used to doing is co-creating that design with you. Your leadership and facilitation in group brainstorming activities such as Design Studio can create safe forums for the entire team to conceptualize your product.

SHIFT: Cross-Functional Teams

For many teams, collaboration is a single-discipline activity. Developers solve problems with other developers, while designers go sit on bean bags, fire up the lava lamps, and "ideate" with their black-turtlenecked brethren (I'm kidding...I love designers!).

The ideas born of single-discipline collaborations are single-faceted. They don't reflect the broader perspective of the team, which can illuminate a wider range of needs, such as the needs of the customer, the business, or the technology. Worse, working this way requires discipline-based teams to explain their work to one another. Too often, the result is a heavy reliance on detailed documentation.

Lean UX requires cross-functional collaboration. By creating interaction between product managers, developers, QA engineers, designers, and marketers, you put everyone on the same page. Equally important: you put everyone on the same level. No single discipline dictates to the other. All are working toward a common goal. Allow your designers to attend "developer meetings" and vice versa. In fact, just have team meetings.

We've known how important cross-functional collaboration is for a long time. Robert Dailey's study from the late 1970s, "The Role of Team and Task Characteristics in R & D Team Collaborative Problem Solving and Productivity,"[1] found a link between a team's problem solving productivity and what he called "four predictors": task certainty, task interdependence, team size, and team cohesiveness. Keep your team cohesive by breaking down the discipline-based boundaries.

---

1   Dailey, 1978, *Management Science*, vol. 24, no. 15, 1579–1588.

SHIFT: Small Teams

Larger groups of people are less efficient than smaller ones. This makes intuitive sense. But less obvious is this: a smaller team must work on smaller problems. This small size makes it easier to maintain the discipline needed to produce minimum viable products. Break your big teams into what Amazon.com founder Jeff Bezos famously called "two-pizza teams" (*http://www.fastcompany.com/50106/inside-mind-jeff-bezos*). If the team needs more than two pizzas to make a meal, it's too big.

SHIFT: Workspace

Break down the physical barriers that prevent collaboration. Co-locate your teams and create workspaces for them that keep everyone visible and accessible. Make space for your team to put their work up on walls and other work surfaces. Nothing is more effective then walking over to a colleague, showing some work, discussing, sketching, exchanging ideas, understanding facial expressions and body language, and reaching a resolution on a thorny topic.

When you co-locate people, create cross-functional groupings. That means removing team members from the comforts of their discipline's "hideout." It's amazing how even one cubicle wall can hinder conversation between colleagues.

Open workspaces allow team members to see each other and to easily reach out when questions arise. Some teams have gone as far as putting their desks on wheels so they can relocate closer to the team members with whom they're collaborating on that particular day. Augment these open spaces with breakout rooms where the teams can brainstorm. Wall-sized whiteboards or painting the walls with whiteboard paint provides many square feet of discussion space. In short, remove the physical obstacles between your team members. Your space planners may not like it at first, but your stakeholders will thank you.

If co-location is not an option, give teams the tools they need to communicate. These include things like video conferencing software (e.g., Skype) and smart boards, but also plane tickets to meet each other in the flesh every now and again. It's amazing what one or two in-person meetings a year will do to team morale.

SHIFT: No More Heroes

On the teams that I've worked with to date, it hasn't been developers who have pushed back on Lean UX. It is designers who have resisted the most. The biggest reason? Many designers want to be *heroes*.

In an environment in which designers create beautiful deliverables, they can attain a heroic aura. Requirements go in one end of the design machine and gorgeous artwork makes its way out. People "ooh" and "aah" when the design is unveiled. Designers have thrived on these reactions (both informal and formalized as awards) for many years.

I'm not suggesting that all of these designs are superficial. Schooling, formal training, experience, and a healthy dose of inspiration go into every Photoshop document designers create—and often the results are smart, well-considered, and valuable. However, those glossy deliverables can drive bad corporate decisions. They can bias judgment specifically because their beauty is so persuasive. Awards are based on the aesthetics of the designs (rather than the outcome of the work), hiring decisions are made on the sharpness of wireframes, and compensation depends on the brand names attached to each of the portfolio pieces.

The creators of these documents are heralded as thought leaders and elevated to the top of the experience design field. But can a single design hero be responsible for the success of the user experience, the business, and the team? Should one person be heralded as the sole reason for an initiative's success?

In short, no!

For Lean UX to succeed in your organization, all types of contributors—designers and nondesigners—must collaborate broadly. This change can be hard for some, especially for visual designers with a background in interactive agencies. In those contexts, the Creative Director is untouchable. In Lean UX, the only thing that's untouchable is customer insight.

Lean UX literally has no time for heroes. The entire concept of design as hypothesis immediately dethrones notions of heroism; as a designer you must expect that many of the your ideas will fail in testing. Heroes don't admit failure. But Lean UX designers embrace it as part of the process.

No More BDUF, Baby

In the Agile community, you sometimes hear people talk about Big Design Up Front, or BDUF. I've been advocating moving away from BDUF for years. But it wasn't always that way.

In the early 2000s, I was a user interface designer at AOL, working on a new browser. The team was working on coming up with ways to innovate upon existing browser feature sets. But they always had to wait to implement anything until I'd created the appropriate mockups, specifications, and flow diagrams that described these new ideas.

One developer got tired of waiting for me and started implementing some of these ideas before the documents were complete. Boy, was I upset! How could he have gone ahead without me? How could he possibly know what to build? What if it was wrong or didn't work? He'd have to rewrite all the code!

Turned out that the work he did allowed us to see some of these ideas much sooner than before. It gave us a glimpse into the actual product experience and allowed us to quickly iterate our designs to be more usable and feasible. From that moment on, we relaxed our BDUF requirements, especially as we pushed into features that required animations and new UI patterns.

The irony of the team's document dependency and the "inspiration" it triggered in that developer was not lost on us. In fact, at the end of the project, I was given a mock award for inspiring "undocumented creativity" in a teammate.

The 'Rogue Developer' award for inspiring undocumented creativity in engineers

is hereby granted to:

Jeff Gothelf

for outstanding performance and lasting contribution to

AOL Explorer

Awarded: August 4, 2005

AOL Explorer Team

Figure 8-1. *My "award" for inspiring undocumented creativity in engineers.*

SHIFT: Speed First, Aesthetics Second

Jason Fried, CEO of 37Signals, once said "Speed first, aesthetics second" (*https://twitter.com/jasonfried/status/23923974217*). He wasn't talking about compromising quality. He was talking about editing his ideas and process down to the core. In Lean UX, working quickly means generating many artifacts. Don't waste time debating which type of artifact to create, and don't waste time polishing them to perfection. Instead, use the one that will take the least amount of time to create and communicate to your team. Remember, these artifacts are a transient part of the project—like a conversation. Get it done. Get it out there. Discuss. Move on.

Aesthetics—in the visual design sense—are an essential part of a finished product and experience. The fit and finish of these elements make a critical contribution to brand, emotional experience, and professionalism. At the visual design refinement stage of the process, putting in the effort to obsess over this layer of presentation makes a lot of sense. However, putting in this level of polish and effort into the early stage artifacts—wireframes, sitemaps, and workflow diagrams—is a waste of time.

By sacrificing the perfection of intermediate design artifacts, your team will get to market faster and learn more quickly which elements of the whole experience (design, workflow, copy, content, performance, value propositions, etc.) are working for the users and which aren't. And you'll be more willing to change and rework your ideas if you've put less effort into presenting them.

SHIFT: Value Problem Solving

Lean UX makes us ask hard questions about how we value design.

If you're a designer reading this, you've probably asked yourself a question that often comes up when speed trumps aesthetic perfection:

> *If my job is now to put out concepts instead of finished ideas, every idea I produce feels half-assed. In fact, I feel like I'm "going for the bronze." Nothing I produce is ever finished. Nothing is indicative of the kind of products I am capable of designing. I am putting out bronze-medal work—on purpose! How can I feel pride and ownership for designs that are simply not done?*

For some designers, Lean UX threatens what they see as their collective body of work, their portfolio, and perhaps even their future employability. These emotions are based on what many hiring managers have valued to date—sexy deliverables. Rough sketches, "version one" of a project, and other low-fidelity artifacts are not the makings of a "killer portfolio," but all of that is now changing.

Although your organization must continue to value aesthetics, polish, and attention to detail, the ability to think fast and build shared understanding must get a promotion. Designers can demonstrate their problem solving skills by illustrating the path they took to get from idea to validated learning to experience. In doing so, they'll demonstrate their deep worth as designers. Organizations that seek out and reward problem solvers will attract—and be attracted to—those designers.

Shift: UX Debt

It's often the case that teams working in agile processes do not actually go back to improve the user interface of the software. But, as the saying goes, "it's not iterative if you only do it once." Teams need to make a commitment to continuous improvement, and that means not simply refactoring code and addressing technical debt but also reworking and improving user interfaces. Teams must embrace the concept of UX debt and make a commitment to continuous improvement of the user experience.

James O'Brien, an interaction designer working in London, describes what happened when his team started tracking UX debt in the same way the team tracked technical debt: "The effect was dramatic. Once we presented [rework] as debt, all opposition fell away. Not only was there no question of the debt not being paid down, but it was consistently prioritized."[2]

To use the concept of UX debt, write stories to capture a gap analysis between where the experience is today and where you'd like it to be. Add these stories to your backlog. Advocate for them.

SHIFT: Agencies Are in the Deliverables Business

Applying Lean UX in an interactive agency is no small challenge. Most agencies are set up in ways that make it difficult to implement Lean UX, which is based on cross-functional collaboration and outcome-focused management. The basic agency business model is simple, after all: clients pay for deliverables, not outcomes. But agency culture is a huge obstacle as well. The culture of hero design is strong in places that elevate individuals to positions such as Executive Creative Director. Cross-disciplinary collaboration can also be difficult in big agencies, where processes and "project phases" encourage deliverables and departmental silos.

Perhaps the most challenging obstacle is the client's expectation to "throw it over the wall" to the agency, then see the results when they're ready. Collaboration between client and agency in this case can be limited to

---

2 Private correspondence

uninformed and unproductive critique that is based on personal bias, poli-tics, and CYA.

To make Lean UX work in an agency, everyone involved in an engage-ment must focus on maximizing two factors: increasing collaboration between client and agency, and working to change the focus from outputs to outcomes.

Some agencies attempt to focus on outcomes by experimenting with a move away from fixed-scope and deliverable-based contracts. Instead, their engagements are based on simple time-and materials agreements, or, more radically, on outcome-based contracts. In either case, the team is freed to spend their time iterating towards a specified goal, not just a deliverable. Clients give up the illusion of control that a deliverables-based contract offers but gain a freedom to pursue meaningful and high-quality solutions that are defined in terms of outcomes, not feature lists.

To increase collaboration, agencies can try to break down the walls that separate them from their clients. Clients can be pulled in to the process earlier and more frequently. Check-ins can be constructed around less for-mal milestones. And collaborative work sessions can be arranged so that both agency and client benefit from the additional insight, feedback, and collaboration with one another.

These are not easy transformations—neither for the agency nor the client who hires it—but it is the model under which the best products get built.

A Quick Note about Development Partners

In agency relationships, software development teams (either at the agency, at the client, or a third-party team) are often treated as outsiders and often brought in at the end of a design phase. It's imperative that you change this tradition: development partners must participate through the life of the project—and not as passive observers. Instead, you should seek to have software development start as early as possible. Again, you are look-ing to create a deep and meaningful collaboration with the entire project team—and to do that, you must actually be working side by side with the developers.

SHIFT: Working with Third-Party Vendors

Third-party software development vendors pose a big challenge to Lean UX methods. If a portion of your work is outsourced to a third-party vendor—regardless of the location of the vendor—the Lean UX process is more likely to break down. The contractual relationship with these vendors can make the flexibility that Lean UX requires difficult to achieve.

When working with third-party vendors, try to create projects based on time and materials. Doing so will make it possible for you to create a flexible relationship with your development partner, which you need in order to respond to the changes that are part of the Lean UX process. Remember, you are building software to learn, and that learning will cause your plans to change. Plan for that change, and structure your vendor relationships around it.

SHIFT: Documentation Standards

Many organizations have strict documentation standards that help them meet both internal as well as external and regulatory compliance. Regardless of the value these documents bring to the team, the organization demands that these be created in a certain way and within certain guidelines. Attempting to circumvent this step will inevitably lead to rework, delays, and dissatisfaction with your work performance.

This situation is exactly when, as designer and coach Lane Halley put it, you "lead with conversation, and trail with documentation." The basic philosophies and concepts of Lean UX can be executed within these environments—conversation, collaborative problem solving, sketching, experimentation, and so on—during the early parts of the project lifecycle. As hypotheses are proven and design directions solidify, transition back from Lean UX to the documentation standard your company requires. Use this documentation for the exact reason your company demands: to capture decision history and inform future teams working on this product. Don't let it prevent you from making the right product decisions.

SHIFT: Be Realistic about Your Environment

Change is scary. The Lean UX approach brings with it a lot of change. Change can be especially disconcerting for managers who have been in their position for a while and are comfortable in their current role. Some managers may be threatened by proposals to work in a new way, which could result negative consequences for you. In these situations, try asking for forgiveness rather than permission. Try out some ideas and prove their value via quantifiable successes. Whether you saved time and money on the project or put out a more successful update than ever before, these achievements can help make your case. If your manager still doesn't see the value in working this way and you believe your organization is progressing down a path of continued "blind design," perhaps it's time to consider alternative employment.

SHIFT: Managing Up and Out

Lean UX gives teams a lot of freedom to pursue effective solutions. It does this by stepping away from a product roadmap approach, instead empowering teams to discover the features they think will best serve the business. But abandoning the product roadmap has a cost—it removes a key tool that the business uses to coordinate the activity of teams. So with the freedom to pursue your agenda comes a responsibility to communicate that agenda.

You must constantly reach out to members of your organization who are not currently involved in your work to make sure they're aware of what's coming down the pike. This communication will also make you aware of what others are planning and help you coordinate. Customer service managers, marketers, parallel business units, and sales teams all benefit from knowing what the product organization is up to. By reaching out to them proactively, you allow them to do their jobs better. In return, they will be far less resistant to the changes your product designs are making.

Two valuable lessons to ensure smoother validation cycles:

- There are always other departments that are affected by your work. Ignore them at your peril.

- Ensure that customers are aware of any significant upcoming changes and allow them to opt out (at least temporarily).

A Last Word

Just as we were putting the final touches on this chapter, we got an email from a colleague. Sometimes it can feel impossible to change the entrenched habits of an organization. So I was delighted to receive this email, which I've excerpted for you here, in which Emily Holmes, Director of K12 UX at Hobsons, describes the changes she's made in her organization:

I think a lot of enterprise companies struggle to figure out the best way to implement these techniques. We initially got a great deal of resistance that we couldn't do Lean UX because we're "not a startup," but of course that's really not true.

We brought in a coach to help reinforce with the team our goal of moving our development process toward a Lean UX methodology (it can help to have an outside voice to reinforce what's being said internally), and since then we've made good progress. In less than a year, our team structure has moved from this:

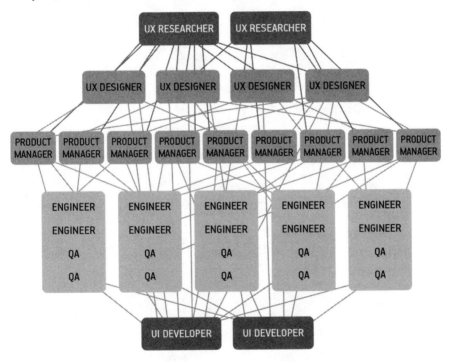

To this:

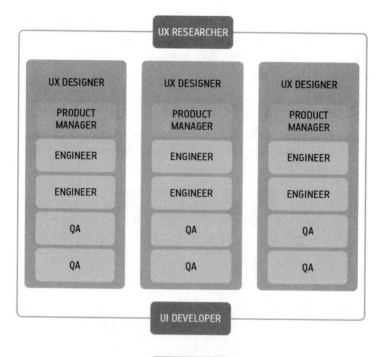

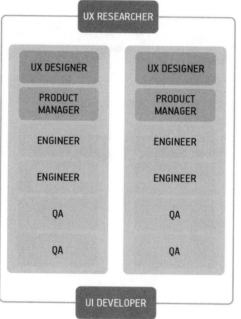

I have introduced the following system for helping our teams internalize what needs to happen as we move through the discovery phase of a project, so that we don't skip any steps and everyone can begin to understand why this thought process needs to happen.

It requires ongoing coaching on my part, and we haven't completely mastered it yet, but it is really helping to get the full team in sync and speaking the same language. That's no small feat, as our team includes people who are accustomed to business analysis, technical specs, and waterfall development. It's a little bit fun, so people don't feel too resentful about having to change old habits. And it definitely helps us fight the "monsters" that have traditionally been problematic for our organization.

I believe a lot of the things that are working for us could be applied to other enterprise organizations quite successfully.

I believe that, too, and I hope that the shifts and principles I've outlined in this chapter will help guide you.

Conclusion

Lean UX is the evolution of product design. It blends the best interaction design techniques with the scientific method to create products that are easy to use, beautiful, and measurably successful. By blending the ideas behind Lean Startup, Agile software development, and design thinking, this approach takes the bloat and uncertainty out of product design and pushes it toward an objectively grounded result. I hope the tactics, strategies, and case studies in this book were useful to you. I am eager to continue the conversation beyond the book and would love to hear from you as you set out to build your Lean UX teams. As you succeed and as you fail, let me know. I want to treat this book as a snapshot in time and use all of your insights to continue to push for better design, team dynamics, and success. Email me at *jeff@jeffgothelf.com* or email Josh at *josh@joshuaseiden.com* with your stories. We look forward to hearing from you.

Index

MVPs (Minimum Viable Products)
about, 7, 55–56
creating, 57–65
focus of, 56–57
hybrids, 69
non-prototype, 69
prototypes, 66–69

N

non-protoype MVPs
about, 68–69
types of, 69

O

O'Brien, James, 117
OmniGraffle program, 62
onsite feedback surveys, 87–89
organizational shifts
about, 109–110
BDUF, 114–115
change environment and, 119
cross-functional teams, 112
designer skills, 111–112
development partners, 118
documentation standards, 119
heros, 114
interactive agencies, 117–118
outcomes, 110–111
product roadmaps, 120
roles, 111
small teams, 113
speed and aesthetics, 116
third-party vendors, 118–119
UX debt, 117
value problem solving, 116–117
workspace, 113
outcome-focused teams, 105
outcomes
creating, 17, 25–26
defined, 8, 18
Knowsy case study, 105
organizational shifts in, 110–111
outliers, parking lot for, 81
outputs, defined, 8

P

paper prototypes, 59–60, 104
parking lot for outliers, 81
patterns, identifying, 81, 82
permission to fail, 11–12

personas
about, 25, 26
brainstorming, 29
proto-personas, 26–29
Petroff, Greg, 43–44
Poehler, Amy, 33
Pop Prototyping on Paper tool, 62
presentation and critique (Design
Studio), 39
previews of prototypes, 66
principles of Lean UX
batch size concept, 9
continuous discovery, 9
cross-functional teams, 7–8
externalizing work, 10–11
GOOB, 9–10
learning over growth, 11
making over analysis, 11
permission to fail, 11–12
problem-focused teams, 8
progress equals outcomes, 8
refocusing design process, 12–13
removing waste, 8–9
shared understanding, 10
team-based mentality, 10
team sizes, 8
prioritizing
assumptions, 22
ideas, 58
proactive communication, 106
problem definition and constraints
(Design Studio), 38
problem-focused teams, 8
problem statements
about, 19
elements of, 20
problem statement templates, 20
product-development lifecycle
Lean Startup method and, 7
Lean UX in, XIV
software distribution in, 3
product roadmaps, 120
proto-personas
about, 26–27
creation process for, 29
formats for drawing, 28–29
prototype MVPs
testing, 66
usage considerations, 66–67
prototypes
about, 59
choosing tools for, 59
clickable wireframe, 61–65, 84

W

waste removal, 8–9, 55
waterfall model, 8, 98
Webtrends Optimize, 89
wikis as style guides, 41, 49
wireframes
    clickable, 61–65, 84
    low-fidelity prototypes, 61–63
    mid- and high-fidelity prototypes,
        64–65
    static, 83–84
work, externalizing, 10–11
workspace in organizational shifts, 113

Y

Yeoh, Cheryl, 70

Have it your way.

Get even more for your money.

Join the O'Reilly Community, and register the O'Reilly books you own. It's free, and you'll get:

- $4.99 ebook upgrade offer
- 40% upgrade offer on O'Reilly print books
- Membership discounts on books and events
- Free lifetime updates to ebooks and videos
- Multiple ebook formats, DRM FREE
- Participation in the O'Reilly community
- Newsletters
- Account management
- 100% Satisfaction Guarantee

Signing up is easy:

1. **Go to: oreilly.com/go/register**
2. **Create an O'Reilly login.**
3. **Provide your address.**
4. **Register your books.**

Note: English-language books only

To order books online:

oreilly.com/store

For questions about products or an order:

orders@oreilly.com

To sign up to get topic-specific email announcements and/or news about upcoming books, conferences, special offers, and new technologies:

elists@oreilly.com

For technical questions about book content:

booktech@oreilly.com

To submit new book proposals to our editors:

proposals@oreilly.com

O'Reilly books are available in multiple DRM-free ebook formats. For more information:

oreilly.com/ebooks

Spreading the knowledge of innovators   oreilly.com